Chinese Programme

D0992586

TRAVEL IN CHINESE

旅游汉语 ❸

《旅游汉语》节目组 编

外语教学与研究出版社
FOREIGN LANGUAGE TEACHING AND RESEARCH PRESS
北京　BEIJING

图书在版编目(CIP)数据

旅游汉语.3 /《旅游汉语》节目组编. —北京：外语教学与研究出版社，2010.1
ISBN 978-7-5600-9295-9

Ⅰ．①旅··· Ⅱ．①旅··· Ⅲ．①旅游－汉语－口语－对外汉语教学－教材 Ⅳ．①H195.4

中国版本图书馆CIP数据核字(2010)第020176号

出 版 人：于春迟
责任编辑：颜丽娜
装帧设计：孙莉明
出版发行：外语教学与研究出版社
社　　址：北京市西三环北路19号（100089）
网　　址：http://www.fltrp.com
印　　刷：北京华联印刷有限公司
开　　本：787×1092 1/16
印　　张：12.25
版　　次：2010年5月第1版 2010年5月第1次印刷
书　　号：ISBN 978-7-5600-9295-9
定　　价：75.00元
＊　　＊　　＊
购书咨询：(010)88819929　　　电子邮箱：club@fltrp.com
如有印刷、装订质量问题出版社负责调换
联系电话：(010)61207896　　　电子邮箱：zhijian@fltrp.com
制售盗版必究 举报查实奖励
版权保护办公室举报电话：(010)88817519
物料号：192950001

《旅游汉语》出版人员名单

Consultant: Zhang Changming
顾问：张长明

Programme Designers: Sheng Yilai Wang Xi
总策划：盛亦来　王晰

Chief Editor: Lai Yunhe
主编：来云鹤

Text Writers: Xin Ping Mark Rowswell (Canada)
撰稿：辛平　大山（加）

Translators: Cheng Lei (Australia) Zhu Xiaomeng
翻译：成蕾（澳）朱晓萌

出版说明

　　近年来，来华旅游、观光的外国朋友越来越多，为满足他们学习汉语、了解中国文化的需要，中国中央电视台英语频道基于多年汉语教学节目的编导经验，特别策划制作了一栏精品汉语教学节目——《旅游汉语》。中央电视台组织经验丰富的对外汉语教学专家进行教学内容的设计与编写，并特邀在中国家喻户晓的大山担任主讲。本节目在中央电视台首播后，收视率一直名列前茅，反响热烈，很多远在海外的观众希望能早日出版该节目的光盘以及配套教材。

　　应广大学习者的要求，中央电视台首先在黄金时间安排重播该节目，并与外语教学与研究出版社联合策划，推出了《旅游汉语》节目的系列配套教材和DVD光盘。

　　本系列教材以一个家庭在中国的生活为主线，强调语言与文化相结合，内容充实、实用性强，在华日常生活中的衣食住行、风俗习惯、旅游常识、景区介绍都包含在其中，主持人大山风趣幽默的语言也给节目增添了许多亮点。

　　配套教材共分五册，每册附DVD光盘两张。每课正文分为以下六个主要部分：课文及英语译文、生词、重点词语注释、文化背景、语言点、句型及替换练习。

　　教材内容由浅入深，由易而难，五册书难度逐级递升，适用于所有以英语为中介语学习汉语的初级读者。学习者可以根据自己的实际汉语水平和需要选择适当的分册开始学习，配合教材并反复学习DVD光盘的内容，以期达到短期内提高汉语口语水平的目的。

外语教学与研究出版社

ontents

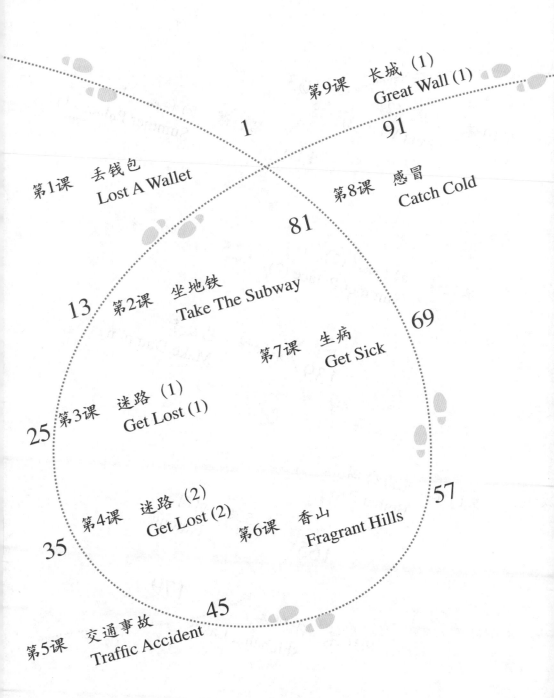

Contents

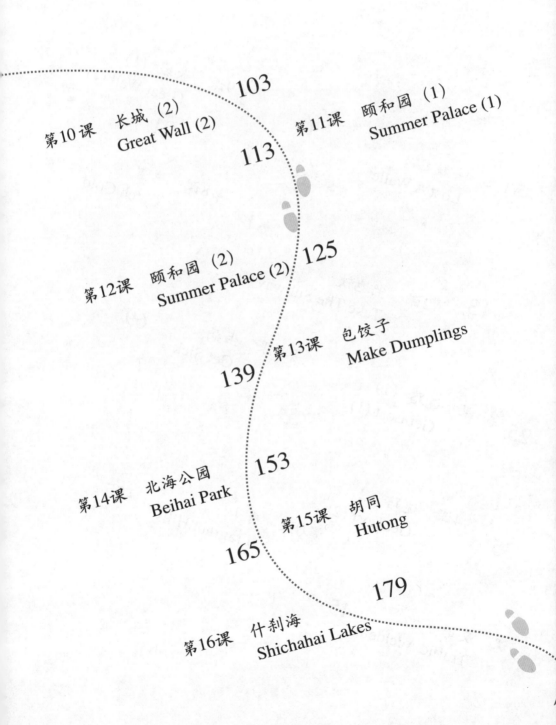

丢钱包
Lost A Wallet

课文

	Xiǎo jié	Zěn me fēi bù qǐ lái ya
	小 杰：	怎 么 飞 不 起 来 呀？

Huáng Rén háo　Nǐ fàng diǎnr xiàn　Kuài pǎo　 zài fàng xiàn
黄 人 豪：你 放 点儿 线。 快 跑， 再 放 线，

duì　wǎng wǒ zhè biānr pǎo
对， 往 我 这 边儿 跑。

Xiǎo jié　Hái shi bù xíng
小 杰：还 是 不 行 。

Huáng Rén háo　Xiàn zài fēng tài xiǎo le　 děng yí huìr　yǒu fēng de
黄 人 豪：现 在 风 太 小 了， 等 一 会儿 有 风 的

shí hou wǒ men zài fàng ba
时 候 我 们 再 放 吧。

Xiǎo jié　Méi xiǎng dào fēng zheng jìng rán zhè me nán fàng
小 杰：没 想 到 风 筝 竟 然 这 么 难 放。

黄 人豪： Bié xiè qì ma yí huìr wǒ men zài shì shi
别 泄气嘛，一 会儿 我 们 再试试。

小 杰： Bà ba wǒ kě le
爸爸，我 渴了。

黄 人豪： Bà gěi nǐ mǎi shuǐ qù Ai wǒ qián bāo ne
爸给你买水去。哎，我钱 包呢？

小 杰： Nǐ gāng cái mǎi fēng zheng de shí hou hái yòng lái
你 刚才买风 筝 的时候还用 来
zhe ne
着呢。

黄 人豪： Duì a wǒ míng míng jì de qián bāo jiù fàng zài
对啊，我明 明记得钱包就放在
zhè ge kǒu dai li le kě xiàn zài zěn me méi
这个口袋里了，可现在怎么没
yǒu le
有了？

小 杰： Huì bú huì shì wǒ men gāng cái pǎo lái pǎo qù pǎo
会不会是我们刚才跑来跑去跑
diū le
丢了？

黄 人豪： Yǒu kě néng kě àn shuō bú huì ya
有可能，可按说不会呀。

小 杰： Wǒ men shùn zhe zhǎo zhao ba
我们顺着找找吧。

黄 人豪： Zǒu
走。

黄 人豪： Xiǎo jié a béng zài zhè li zhǎo le gū jì méi
小杰啊，甭在这里找了，估计没
diū zài zhèr
丢在这儿。

小 杰： Bà ba wǒ men gān cuì qù bào àn ba bǎ nǐ de
爸爸，我们干脆去报案吧，把你的

旅游汉语

shǒu jī gěi wǒ　　wǒ lái bō
手 机 给 我，我 来 拨 911。

Huáng Rén háo　Xiǎo jié　　zài Zhōng guó a　　bú shì bō　　　yīng
黄 人 豪：小 杰，在 中 国 啊，不 是 拨 911，应

gāi shì bō　　　bú guò xiàn zài zài gōng yuán li
该 是 拨 110，不 过 现 在 在 公 园 里，

wǒ men zhǎo bǎo ān jiù xíng le
我 们 找 保 安 就 行 了。

Xiǎo jié　　Bà ba　　nàr　　zhèng hǎo yǒu gè bǎo ān　　wǒ men
小 杰：爸 爸，那 儿 正 好 有 个 保 安，我 们

kuài diǎnr qù ba
快 点 儿 去 吧。

Huáng Rén háo　Zǒu
黄 人 豪：走。

Nǐ hǎo
你 好！

Bǎo ān　　Qǐng wèn nǐ men yǒu shén me shì qing
保 安：请 问 你 们 有 什 么 事 情？

Huáng Rén háo　Wǒ men zài nà bian fàng fēng zheng　　yě jiù yí kè
黄 人 豪：我 们 在 那 边 放 风 筝，也 就 一 刻

zhōng ba　　jiù fā xiàn qián bāo bú jiàn le
钟 吧，就 发 现 钱 包 不 见 了。

Bǎo ān　　Fàng fēng zheng de shí hou　　qián bāo hái zài ma
保 安：放 风 筝 的 时 候，钱 包 还 在 吗？

Huáng Rén háo　Yì zhí fàng fēng zheng lái zhe　　méi zěn me zhù yì
黄 人 豪：一 直 放 风 筝 来 着，没 怎 么 注 意。

Bú guò mǎi fēng zheng de shí hou qián bāo hái zài ne
不 过 买 风 筝 的 时 候 钱 包 还 在 呢。

Bǎo ān　　Zài nǎr　　mǎi de fēng zheng
保 安：在 哪 儿 买 的 风 筝？

Huáng Rén háo　Jiù zài nà biānr　　bù yuǎn
黄 人 豪：就 在 那 边 儿，不 远。

Bǎo ān　　Shì shén me yàng de qián bāo
保 安：是 什 么 样 的 钱 包？

4

黄人豪：是个方形的皮钱夹，颜色就和这条裤子差不多。

保安：里边都有什么？

黄人豪：大约两百块钱，一张信用卡和一些出租车的发票。

保安：你叫什么名字？

黄人豪：黄人豪。

保安：你看这个是不是你的？刚才有人送过来了，你把钱包落在卖风筝的柜台上了。

黄人豪：就是这个。谢谢你了啊。

Xiaojie:	Why doesn't it fly?
Huang Renhao:	Let out the string, quick, let out some more, yes, run towards me!
Xiaojie:	No, it still doesn't work.
Huang Renhao:	The wind's a bit light now, wait till it gets stronger.
Xiaojie:	I never thought flying a kite would be this hard.
Huang Renhao:	Don't give up, we'll try again later.
Xiaojie:	Dad, I'm thirsty.
Huang Renhao:	I'll get you something to drink. Hey, where's my wallet?
Xiaojie:	You had it when you bought the kite.
Huang Renhao:	That's right. I clearly remember putting the wallet in this pocket. Why isn't it here now?
Xiaojie:	Could you have lost it when we were running around just now?
Huang Renhao:	Maybe, but I don't think so.
Xiaojie:	Let's look for it here.
Huang Renhao:	Go.

Huang Renhao:	Xiaojie, we should give up looking here. I don't think I lost

it here.

Xiaojie: Dad, let's report it to the police. Give me your mobile phone and I'll call 911.

Huang Renhao: Xiaojie, you don't dial 911, but 110 in China. But since we're in a park, let's just report it to the security guard.

Xiaojie: Hey, dad, there's a security guard over there. Come on, let's go.

Huang Renhao: Let's go.

Hello!

Security Guard: What's wrong?

Huang Renhao: We were flying a kite over there, just about a quarter of an hour ago. Then I found my wallet was missing.

Security Guard: Did you have the wallet when you were flying the kite?

Huang Renhao: We were flying the kite and didn't really notice. But I remember I used it to buy the kite.

Security Guard: Where did you buy the kite?

Huang Renhao: Just up ahead, not far.

Security Guard: What sort of wallet is it?

Huang Renhao: It's a square leather wallet, the colour of this pair of trousers.

Security Guard: What's in it?

Huang Renhao: About two hundred *yuan*, a credit card and some taxi receipts.

Security Guard: What's your name?

Huang Renhao: Huang Renhao.

Security Guard: Take a look at this, is it yours? Somebody handed it in just now. You left it on the counter where you got the kite.

Huang Renhao: That's it. Thank you!

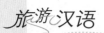

1.	线	xiàn	名	string
2.	风筝	fēng zheng	名	kite
3.	竟然	jìng rán	副	unexpectedly
4.	难	nán	形	hard
5.	泄气	xiè qì	动	lose heart
6.	明明	míng míng	副	undoubtedly
7.	甭	béng	副	need not
8.	估计	gū jì	动	estimate
9.	干脆	gān cuì	副	simply
10.	报案	bào àn	动	report a case to the police
11.	手机	shǒu jī	名	mobile phone
12.	公园	gōng yuán	名	park
13.	保安	bǎo ān	名	security guard
14.	注意	zhù yì	动	notice
15.	皮	pí	名	leather
16.	大约	dà yuē	副	about

注释

1. 等一会儿有风的时候我们再放吧。

> Wait a while until there is some wind and then try again. In previous lessons, we learned about this "to do sth. 再 sth. else" pattern, first do something and then do something else.

2. 没想到风筝竟然这么难放。

> I never thought it would be this hard to fly a kite. 竟然 means unexpectedly. You can omit this and have roughly the same meaning, 没想到风筝这么难放. But adding 竟然 adds emphasis and makes the meaning "unexpected" much clearer.

3. 会不会是我们刚才跑来跑去跑丢了？

> Did you lose it when you were running around? 跑来跑去 doesn't necessarily mean you were running, just that you were very busy doing different things in different places. The result is 跑丢了, lost something while you were busy running around.

4. 可按说不会呀。

> Remember we learned 据说, it is said? Here we see a similar expression 按说不会呀, it shouldn't be possible. 按 has a similar meaning to 据, according to.

5. 我们干脆去报案吧。

> Let's just go and file a report with the police or with the authorities. 案 is a case or investigation. 报案 is to report some problem to the authorities, to start an investigation. 干脆 means clear cut or simply. In other words, let's not waste any more time here, let's go right away. This is a useful term, such as in 干脆不要了, forget about it, I don't want it anymore. Xiaojie suggests they dial 911, but that is the emergency number in many western countries. In China, the number you dial for police is 110. For fire emergency, you dial 119. Different countries use different emergency numbers.

6. 是个方形的皮钱夹，颜色就和这条裤子差不多。

> Huang Renhao describes his missing wallet 一个方形的皮钱夹, a square leather bill fold. 夹 is to place between two things, or to press from both sides. 钱夹 is a bill fold, where money is folded between two sides of leather. 颜色就和这条裤子差不多, the colour is similar to this pair of pants. 条 is the measure word for pants. 和 sth. 差不多 means roughly similar to something, not exactly the same. If something was just the same, we would say 和 sth. 一样.

7. 刚才有人送过来了

> Somebody just sent it in. 刚才 indicates that it just happened a short while ago.

文化
背景

Chinese Kites

Rather than talking about the unpleasant business of having lost something, let's focus instead on kites, which were actually invented in China. Even the National Aeronautics and Space Museum in Washington D.C. claims that "the earliest aircraft were the kites of China".

Chinese kites date back over two thousand years. Before the invention of paper, they were originally made with wood and bamboo. Some early kites were used for military purposes and were large enough to carry a man aloft so that he could observe enemy positions. Others were used to send messages.

The Chinese word for kite is 风筝. 筝 is a traditional Chinese musical instrument. In the Tang Dynasty from the 7th to 10th century A.D., people would tie small strips of bamboo that would vibrate and hum in the breeze, sounding something like the 筝.

Today there are over 300 varieties of kites in China. Probably the best place to see them is during the national kite festival held every year in Weifang in Shandong Province.

1. 竟然 unexpectedly

没想到**竟然**在这儿碰到他。
I didn't expect to meet him here.
他**竟然**连这个问题的答案都不知道。
He doesn't even know the answer to this question.

2. 干脆 simply

那位导游非常**干脆**地回答了所有的问题。
That tour guide answered all of the questions very simply and straightforward.
这个问题处理得很**干脆**。
This problem has been solved in a very straightforward manner.

1. V+来+V+去

跑来跑去，走来走去
to run around; to walk around
我们**想来想去**，也不知道到底该怎么办。
We've been thinking this all over the place, but we still don't know what we should do in the end.
替换例句：
我**挑来挑去**，还是没买到合适的衣服。
我拿着地图**看来看去**，还是没找到去机场的路。

2. 和/跟……差不多 not very different

北京的天气和我们那儿的天气差不多。

The weather in Beijing and the weather where we are are about the same.

这种水果的味道跟梨的味道差不多。

This kind of fruit tastes quite a lot like pears.

替换例句：

小王的个头和小李差不多。

北京的物价和上海差不多。

坐地铁

Take The Subway

课文

Biǎo jiě　Wǒ men děi kuài diǎnr le　yào bù gāi gǎn bú shàng
表 姐：我 们 得 快 点儿 了，要 不 该 赶 不 上

zhè chǎng diàn yǐng le
这 场 电 影 了。

Xuě méi　Wǒ hǎo jiǔ méi dào diàn yǐng yuàn kàn diàn yǐng le　hái
雪 梅：我 好 久 没 到 电 影 院 看 电 影 了，还

yuǎn ma
远 吗？

Biǎo jiě　Bù yuǎn le　ai　Xuě méi　nǐ de bāo zěn me kāi
表 姐：不 远 了，哎，雪 梅，你 的 包 怎 么 开

zhe ne
着 呢？

Xuě méi　Guài le　wǒ míng míng lā shàng le　zěn me kāi
雪 梅：怪 了，我 明 明 拉 上 了，怎 么 开

le ne
了 呢？

Xuě méi　A　wǒ de qián bāo méi yǒu le
雪 梅：啊，我 的 钱 包 没 有 了！

Biǎo jiě　Nà qí tā dōng xi ne
表 姐：那 其 他 东 西 呢？

Xuě méi　Wǒ kàn kan　hù zhào　bǐ jì běn　dōu zài
雪 梅：我 看 看，护 照 、笔 记 本 …… 都 在，

zhǐ yǒu qián bāo diū le
只 有 钱 包 丢 了。

Biǎo jiě　Zài shén me dì fang diū de ne
表 姐：在 什 么 地 方 丢 的 呢？

Xuě méi　Bú shì gōng gòng qì chē shang jiù shì dì tiě li　Wǒ
雪 梅：不 是 公 共 汽 车 上 就 是 地 铁 里？我

zěn me yì diǎnr gǎn jué dōu méi yǒu ne
怎 么 一 点 儿 感 觉 都 没 有 呢？

Biǎo jiě　Bié jí　wǒ men zài zhǎo zhao　Rú guǒ bù xíng de
表 姐：别 急，我 们 再 找 找 。如 果 不 行 的

huà　wǒ men zài qù pài chū suǒ bào àn
话，我 们 再 去 派 出 所 报 案。

Tóng shì　Ai　Xuě méi　wǒ dǎ lǎo yuǎn jiù kàn jiàn nǐ le　gěi
同 事：哎，雪 梅，我 打 老 远 就 看 见 你 了，给

nǐ dǎ le bàn tiān zhāo hu nǐ yě méi kàn jiàn wǒ　Zhè
你 打 了 半 天 招 呼 你 也 没 看 见 我。这

wèi shì
位 是 ……？

Xuě méi　Zhè shì wǒ xiān sheng de biǎo jiě　Biǎo jiě　zhè shì
雪 梅：这 是 我 先 生 的 表 姐。表 姐，这 是

wǒ tóng shì　Xiǎo Lǐ
我 同 事，小 李。

Tóng shì　Nǐ men èr wèi shì qù nǎr　a
同 事：你 们 二 位 是 去 哪 儿 啊？

Xuě méi　Bié tí le　běn lái wǒ xiǎng hé biǎo jiě yì qǐ qù kàn
雪 梅：别 提 了，本 来 我 想 和 表 姐 一 起 去 看

diàn yǐng de　kě shì fā xiàn wǒ de qián bāo bú jiàn le
电 影 的，可 是 发 现 我 的 钱 包 不 见 了，

zhè bu zhèng dào chù zhǎo ne
这 不 正 到 处 找 呢！

Biǎo jiě　Yì chū dì tiě kǒu　wǒ jiù fā xiàn tā de bāo kāi le
表 姐：一 出 地 铁 口，我 就 发 现 她 的 包 开 了。

Tóng shì　Nà shì zài dì tiě li diū de ba
同 事：那 是 在 地 铁 里 丢 的 吧。

Xuě méi　Zhè ge shuō bù hǎo　Yě xǔ zài gōng gòng qì chē
雪 梅：这 个 说 不 好。也 许 在 公 共 汽 车

shang jiù yǐ jing diū le
上 就 已 经 丢 了。

Tóng shì　Yào wǒ shuō　nǐ men zuì hǎo hái shi qù pài chū suǒ
同 事：要 我 说，你 们 最 好 还 是 去 派 出 所

bào gè àn ba
报 个 案 吧。

Biǎo jiě　Duì　wǒ men hái shi xiān qù pài chū suǒ ba　Rú guǒ
表 姐：对，我 们 还 是 先 去 派 出 所 吧。如 果

bèi rén jiǎn dào le　tā men yě hǎo tōng zhī wǒ men
被 人 捡 到 了，他 们 也 好 通 知 我 们 。

Xuě méi　Pài chū suǒ lí　zhèr yuǎn ma
雪 梅：派 出 所 离 这 儿 远 吗？

Tóng shì　Bù yuǎn　cóng zhèr wǎng qián zǒu jiù dào le
同 事：不 远，从 这 儿 往 前 走 就 到 了。

Bù rán wǒ péi nǐ men liǎng gè yí kuàir qù ba
不 然 我 陪 你 们 两 个 一 块 儿 去 吧。

Xuě méi　Xiè xie　Dōu guài wǒ bù xiǎo xīn　xiàn zài diàn yǐng
雪 梅：谢 谢！都 怪 我 不 小 心，现 在 电 影

yě kàn bù chéng le
也 看 不 成 了。

Biǎo jiě　Qiáo nǐ shuō de　diū dōng xi zhè shìr　shuí dōu nán
表 姐：瞧 你 说 的，丢 东 西 这 事 儿，谁 都 难

miǎn　Diàn yǐng kàn bù chéng yǒu shén me dà bù liǎo
免 。电 影 看 不 成 有 什 么 大 不 了

de　Zán men zǒu ba
的？咱 们 走 吧。

Cousin: We need to hurry, or we won't make the movie.

Xuemei: I haven't been to a movie at the cinema for ages. Is the cinema far from here?

Cousin: Not far. Hey, Xuemei, why is your bag open?

Xuemei: That's strange. I zipped it closed. How come it's open?

Xuemei: Oh no, my purse is gone!

Cousin: What about your other things?

Xuemei: Let me see. Passport, notebook…all here, just the purse is gone.

Cousin: Where did you lose it?

Xuemei: Either on the bus or on the subway? How come I didn't notice anything?

Cousin: Don't panic, we'll look for it. If we still can't find it, we'll report it to the police.

Colleague: Hey, Xuemei, I saw you a long way back. I kept waving to you but you didn't see me.

Xuemei: This is my husband's cousin. Cousin, this is my colleague Xiao Li.

Colleague: Where are you planning on going?

Xuemei: Don't ask, I was planning to go to a movie with my cousin. But now I've found my purse is missing. We're still looking for it!

Cousin: As soon as we got out of the subway exit, I saw her bag was open.

Colleague: Then you lost it in the subway.

Xuemei: We can't be sure. Maybe it was already lost on the bus.

Colleague: If you ask me, you'd better report it to the police.

Cousin: Yes, let's go to the police station. If someone finds it, they can contact us.

Xuemei: Is the police station far from here?

Colleague: Not far. Go straight ahead. How about I go with you two?

Xuemei: Thank you! It's all my fault for being so careless, now we're going to miss the movie.

Cousin: Don't be silly, we all lose things sometimes. Missing a movie's not a big deal. Let 's go.

生词

1.	电影	diàn yǐng	名	movie
2.	电影院	diàn yǐng yuàn	名	theatre, cinema
3.	拉	lā	动	zip
4.	笔记本	bǐ jì běn	名	notebook
5.	不是…… 就是……	bú shì…jiù shì…		if it's not this, it must be that
6.	公共汽车	gōng gòng qì chē	名	bus
7.	地铁	dì tiě	名	subway
8.	派出所	pài chū suǒ	名	police station
9.	招呼	zhāo hu	名	greeting
10.	本来	běn lái	副	originally
11.	到处	dào chù	名	everywhere
12.	捡	jiǎn	动	pick up
13.	难免	nán miǎn	副	hard to avoid

注释

1. 怪了，我明明拉上了。
- That's strange, I'm sure I closed it. 怪了 is like 奇怪, strange. 明明 means that something is obvious, or you are sure of something. 拉 is to pull, or in this case, to zip up a zipper.

2. 不是公共汽车上就是地铁里。
- If it wasn't on the bus, it must have been on the subway. Of course, this sentence by itself could either be in the past or present tense. Based on the context of the dialogue, we translate it into English as being in the past tense.

3. 我怎么一点儿感觉都没有呢？
- How could it be that I didn't feel anything? 一点儿 sth. 都没有 is another useful pattern, to not have the slightest amount of something.

4. 这个说不好。
- That's hard to say. She can't be sure.

5. 要我说，你们最好还是去派出所报个案吧。
- In my view, it would be best if you went to report to the police. 要我说 is like saying if you ask me. In this sentence, 还是 is used to indicate a suggestion or recommendation.

6. 他们也好通知我们。
- Here, 好 is used to indicate so that, in order that.

7. 瞧你说的，丢东西这事儿，谁都难免。
- 瞧你说的 is a colloquial expression to indicate that you disagree with what has been said. Literally, look at what you've said. 丢东西这事儿，谁都难免。 As for losing things, it could happen to anybody, it's hard to avoid. 难免 literally means difficult to avoid.

Beijing Subway

The Beijing subway dates back to the 1960's but is undergoing rapid development right now. Originally, there were two subway lines. A circular line that follows under the 2nd ring road. This was originally the location of the Beijing city wall, and many of the intersections today still retain the original place names. That's why many of the subway stops are places called 门 (gate), like 前门, the front gate, just south of Tian'anmen.

A second original subway line travels along an east-west route, following under Chang'an Blvd.. This is the wide avenue that passes right in front of Tian'anmen Square. In fact, there are two subway exits on the east and west side of the square. Chang'an Blvd. changes names as it goes from the far eastern side of Beijing to right near the Western Hills on the other side of Beijing.

In recent years, old lines have been expanded and new lines are being built. Some of these lines go up to the Summer Palace, or around the northern suburbs of Beijing. Another line cuts straight through the city from north to south. These lines are often called 轻轨, light rail transit, rather than 地铁 (subway), because they travel at least part of their routes elevated above the city rather than underground. By the time the Olympics arrived in 2008, much of this new construction had been finished.

旅游汉语

语言点

1. 明明 something is clearly different

你**明明**知道下午有事，为什么还出去?

You obviously knew that there was something happening this afternoon. Why did you go out?

他**明明**去过那儿，却说他根本没去过。

He's obviously been there before, but he said he'd never been there before.

2. 好 in order that

带上雨衣吧，下雨**好**用。

Bring a raincoat in case it rains.

你留个电话，有事**好**互相联系。

Leave me a phone number so that we can contact each other when we need to.

3. 难免 hard to avoid

朋友之间，看法**难免**有时会不一致。

Even between friends, it's hard to avoid sometimes having different points of view.

你刚开始学习汉语，这样的错误是**难免**的。

You've just started learning Chinese. This kind of mistake is hard to avoid.

句型 及 替换练习

不是……就是…… if it's not this，it must be that

妈妈不是星期六来就是星期日来。

替换例句:

他的衣服不是蓝的就是黑的。

他不是在办公室就是在家，你肯定能找到他。

第 *3* 课

迷路（1）
Get Lost（1）

旅游汉语

课文

Xuě méi　Má fan nǐ wèn yí xiàr　　wǒ men xiǎng qù Běi jīng
雪梅：麻烦你问一下儿，我们想去北京
　　　　Yīn yuè tīng　yīng gāi zěn me zuò chē
　　　　音乐厅，应该怎么坐车？

Lù rén　Běi jīng Yīn yuè tīng　You　nà　lí　zhèr　kě
路人：北京音乐厅？呦，那离这儿可
　　　　bú jìn
　　　　不近。

Xuě méi　Dàn yīng gāi yǒu qù nàr　de gōng gòng qì chē ba
雪梅：但应该有去那儿的公共汽车吧。

Lù rén　Yǒu dào shì yǒu　bú guò děi huàn chē　Nǐ men děi
路人：有倒是有，不过得换车。你们得
　　　　xiān zuò gōng gòng qì chē rán hòu zài huàn chéng dì tiě
　　　　先坐公共汽车然后再换乘地铁。

小杰：Xiǎo jié Zuò jǐ lù gōng gòng qì chē
小杰：坐几路公共汽车？

Lù rén Zuò lù hé lù dōu xíng
路人：坐33路和718路都行。

Xuě méi Xiǎo jié nǐ bāng wǒ jì yí xiàr miǎn de wǒ
雪梅：小杰，你帮我记一下儿，免得我

wàng le
忘了。

Xiǎo jié Méi wèn tí
小杰：没问题。

Xuě méi Zuò dào shén me dì fang huàn dì tiě ne
雪梅：坐到什么地方换地铁呢？

Lù rén Zuò dào Gōng zhǔ fén rán hòu zài huàn dì tiě
路人：坐到公主坟，然后再换地铁。

Xiǎo jié Dì tiě zuò dào nǎr xià chē ne
小杰：地铁坐到哪儿下车呢？

Lù rén Zuò dào Xī dān zhàn xià chē yǐ hòu nǐ men zài dǎ
路人：坐到西单站，下车以后你们再打

ting dǎ ting
听打听。

Xuě méi Xiè xie
雪梅：谢谢。

Xiǎo jié Mā ma chē zhàn zài zhèr kuài guò lái
小杰：妈妈，车站在这儿，快过来。

Xuě méi Zhè me duō lù chē dōu zài zhèr
雪梅：这么多路车都在这儿。

Xiǎo jié Chē lái le kuài guò lái
小杰：车来了，快过来。

Xuě méi Ai nǐ màn diǎnr hái bù zhī dào zhè chē shì wǎng
雪梅：哎，你慢点儿，还不知道这车是往

nǎ ge fāng xiàng kāi de ne
哪个方向开的呢？

Xiǎo jié　Fǎn zhèng shì　　xiān shàng chē zài shuō ba
小 杰： 反 正 是718，先 上 车 再 说 吧。

Xuě méi　Zhè kě bù xíng　děi xiān wèn wen qīng chu
雪 梅： 这 可 不 行，得 先 问 问 清 楚。

Qǐng wèn　　zhè chē shì dào Gōng zhǔ fén ma
请 问，这 车 是 到 公 主 坟 吗？

Děng chē rén　Qù Gōng zhǔ fén　Bú duì　fāng xiàng fǎn le　qù
等 车 人： 去 公 主 坟？不 对，方 向 反 了，去

Gōng zhǔ fén de chē dào mǎ lù duì miàn qù zuò
公 主 坟 的 车 到 马 路 对 面 去 坐。

Xuě méi　Xiè xie　Nǐ kàn　cuò le ba　Nǐ a　duō kuī méi
雪 梅： 谢 谢！你 看，错 了 吧。你 啊，多 亏 没

shàng nà liàng chē　Wǒ de gǎn jué hái shi tǐng zhǔn
上 那 辆 车。我 的 感 觉 还 是 挺 准

ma
嘛！

Xiǎo jié　Hai　xìng kuī méi tīng wǒ de　Yí huìr　hái děi zuò
小 杰： 嗨，幸 亏 没 听 我 的。一 会 儿 还 得 坐

dì tiě　dào shí hou kě bié zuò fǎn le
地 铁，到 时 候 可 别 坐 反 了。

Xuě méi　Wǒ yǐ qián hé nǐ gū mā yì qǐ zuò guo　jué duì méi
雪 梅： 我 以 前 和 你 姑 妈 一 起 坐 过，绝 对 没

wèn tí　Bú guò　Xiǎo jié　nǐ yǐ hòu bù guǎn zuò
问 题。不 过，小 杰，你 以 后 不 管 坐

shén me chē　dōu děi duō wèn wen　miǎn de zuò cuò le
什 么 车，都 得 多 问 问，免 得 坐 错 了。

Xiǎo jié　Ng　wǒ jì zhù le　Mā ma　nǐ kàn duì miàn lái chē
小 杰： 嗯，我 记 住 了。妈 妈，你 看 对 面 来 车

le　wǒ men kuài guò qù
了，我 们 快 过 去。

Xuemei: Sorry to trouble you, we want to go to Beijing Concert Hall. Which bus should we take?

Pedestrian: Beijing Concert Hall? Oh, that's pretty far from here.

Xuemei: There must be a bus that goes there.

Pedestrian: There is, but you have to change. First you take the bus, then change to the subway.

Xiaojie: What number bus?

Pedestrian: You can take either the 33 or 718.

Xuemei: Xiaojie, help me remember this, in case I forget.

Xiaojie: Sure.

Xuemei: Where do we change to the subway?

Pedestrian: Get off at Gongzhufen, then change to the subway.

Xiaojie: Which subway station do we get off at?

Pedestrian: You get off at Xidan station, then ask around.

Xuemei: Thank you.

Xiaojie: Mum, the bus station is here. Come on.

Xuemei: All these different buses stop here.

Xiaojie: The bus is here. Hurry!

Xuemei: Hey, slow down. You don't know which way the bus is going.

Xiaojie: It's the 718, we can get on the bus first.

Xuemei: That won't do, we've got to ask first. Excuse me, does this bus go to Gongzhufen?

Person waiting for bus: To Gongzhufen? No, that's the opposite direction. Buses going to Gongzhufen leave from across the road.

Xuemei: Thanks! See, it was wrong. Thank god we didn't get on that bus. My instinct was right!

Xiaojie: Just as well we didn't do what I said. In a while we'll have to take the subway too. We'd better not go in the wrong direction there.

Xuemei: I've taken it with your aunt before. There's definitely no problem. But remember Xiaojie, no matter what bus you take in the future, it pays to ask around, so you don't go the wrong way.

Xiaojie: OK, I got it. Mum, the bus across the road is here. Let's run for it!

生词

1.	麻烦	má fan	动	bother
2.	音乐厅	yīn yuè tīng	名	concert hall
3.	免得	miǎn de	连	in order to avoid something
4.	打听	dǎ ting	动	ask about
5.	方向	fāng xiàng	名	direction
6.	马路	mǎ lù	名	road
7.	对面	duì miàn	名	opposite side
8.	多亏	duō kuī	动	thanks to
9.	准	zhǔn	形	accurate
10.	幸亏	xìng kuī	副	fortunately
11.	姑妈	gū mā	名	aunt
12.	不管…… 都……	bù guǎn…dōu…		no matter what

注释

1. 你们得先坐公共汽车然后再换乘地铁。

You have to first take a bus, then transfer to the subway. Today we're going to practise this pattern "先 sth., 然后 sth.", first sth. then sth. else.

2. 免得我忘了。

So that I don't forget. 免得 means to avoid something.

3. 下车以后你们再打听打听。

Ask around after you get off the subway. 打听打听 is a more colloquial version of 问问. 打听 is to ask for information.

4. 这么多路车都在这儿。

There are so many bus routes here. 这么多车都在这儿 would mean there are so many cars or buses here. 这么多路车 indicates that you are talking about bus routes, not the buses themselves.

5. 反正是718。

Anyway, it's 718. In other words, don't worry about anything else, at least this is the number we are looking for. 反正 is like anyway, regardless.

6. 去公主坟的车到马路对面去坐。

You should board the bus to 公主坟 on the other side of the road. 对面 is the opposite side. 公主坟 (notice we use the 儿 ending in Beijing) is a major intersection in Beijing. It literally means tomb of the princess. But the tomb or the grave site, if it ever really existed, is no longer there. It's just a place name now.

7. 多亏没上那辆车。

We're lucky we didn't board that bus. 多亏, it's fortunate or lucky.

8. 别坐反了。

Don't take the wrong direction. 坐反了 literally means to sit in the wrong direction or the wrong side. Here 坐 is used as the verb to board or to take (a bus). Xuemei is confident, 绝对没问题, there's absolutely no problem.

Taking a Bus in China

Taking a bus in China is an interesting experience. You should try it at least once. There are nice air-conditioned buses with soft seats and lots of space, then there are the super crowded ones where people are packed in like sardines. But no matter how packed the buses are, people still manage to get on and get off when they need to.

On most buses, the driver doesn't handle fares and tickets. That's done by an attendant who sits near the door. Longer buses will sometimes have a second attendant at the back. If you don't have a monthly pass, you will have to buy a ticket after boarding the bus. Hold on to the small ticket receipt as proof of purchase.

Once I was on a bus that was so crowded that I just didn't think it would be physically possible for me to reach the ticket attendant. So I said to myself, forget about it, 算了吧, I'm only going a few stops anyway. Sure enough, there was a ticket inspector waiting for me when I got off. It just goes to show you being too crowded is not an excuse for not buying a ticket. I had to pay a fine.

Note that when we ask for bus numbers in Chinese, we don't say 几号车. We say 几路车. This specifies that you are asking for the route number, not the license number of a particular bus.

Because there are so many people, most buses will stop at every stop. You don't have to ring a bell to get off, or wave your arms to flag down a bus.

语言点

1. 免得 to avoid something

带上一张地图吧，**免得**迷路。

You should bring a map so that you don't get lost.

你最好给家里打个电话，**免得**妈妈担心。

It would be best for you to call home, so that your mother doesn't become anxious.

2. 多亏 fortunately

多亏我们提前订好了酒店，要不然连住的地方都没有。

Fortunately, we reserved a hotel in advance. Otherwise, we wouldn't even have a place to stay.

多亏我穿了件毛衣，否则这次一定会感冒的。

Fortunately, I wore a sweater. Otherwise, I surely would have caught a cold this time.

句型 及 替换练习

不管……都…… no matter what

不管多累，我都要去爬长城。

No matter how tired, I still want to climb the Great Wall.

替换例句：

不管有多忙，他都坚持每天学一小时汉语。

不管有多热，他都不开空调。

第 4 课

迷路（2）

Get Lost (2)

课文

Xiǎo jié　　Mā ma　　　nǐ huí lái le
小 杰：妈妈，你回来了。

Xuě méi　　Nǐ jiě jie gěi wǒ men jì bāo guǒ lái le
雪 梅：你姐姐给我们寄包裹来了。

Xiǎo jié　　Zhēn de　　shén me dōng xi a　　Qǔ huí lái le ma
小 杰：真的，什么东西啊？取回来了吗？

Xuě méi　　Bù zhī dào　　hái méi qù qǔ ne
雪 梅：不知道，还没去取呢。

Xiǎo jié　　Xiàn zài jiù qù qǔ ba　　zhèng hǎo wǒ yě méi shìr
小 杰：现 在就去取吧，正 好我也没 事儿，

zán men liǎ yí kuàir　　qù
咱 们俩一 块儿去。

Xuě méi　　Xíng a　　　bú guò wǒ děi xiān kàn kan dì tú　　zhǎo
雪 梅：行 啊，不过我得先看看地图，找

zhao yóu jú de wèi zhi
找 邮局的位置。

Xiǎo jié　Bú zhì yú nà me fù zá ba　yǒu wǒ ne
小 杰：不至于那么复杂吧， 有 我 呢。

Xuě méi　Bié chuī niú le　Hǎo　chū fā　Chū mén zuǒ guǎi
雪 梅：别 吹 牛 了。好， 出 发！ 出 门 左 拐。

Xiǎo jié　Yì zhí wǎng qián zǒu jiù dào le ma
小 杰：一 直 往 前 走 就 到 了 吗？

Xuě méi　Zǒu dào dì sān gè lù kǒu　zài guǎi wānr
雪 梅：走 到 第 三 个 路 口， 再 拐 弯儿。

Xiǎo jié　Zhè jiù shì dì sān gè lù kǒu le
小 杰：这 就 是 第 三 个 路 口 了。

Xuě méi　Jiù zài zhèr wǎng yòu guǎi　guǎi guò qù yǐ hòu hěn
雪 梅：就 在 这儿 往 右 拐， 拐 过 去 以 后 很

kuài jiù dào le
快 就 到 了。

Xiǎo jié　Mā ma　wǒ men zǒu de kě bú jìn le　zěn me hái méi
小 杰：妈 妈， 我 们 走 得 可 不 近 了， 怎 么 还 没

kàn jiàn yóu jú de yǐngr ne
看 见 邮 局 的 影儿 呢？

Xuě méi　Wǒ yě yǒu diǎnr　nà mènr　àn shuō gāi dào le
雪 梅：我 也 有 点儿 纳 闷儿， 按 说 该 到 了，

nǐ lái kàn dì tú
你 来 看 地 图。

Xiǎo jié　Zhè ge dì tú zhēn fù zá　wǒ kàn jí shǐ shì Zhōng
小 杰：这 个 地 图 真 复 杂， 我 看 即 使 是 中

guó rén kǒng pà yě kàn bù dǒng　wǒ men hái shi wèn
国 人 恐 怕 也 看 不 懂， 我 们 还 是 问

wen bié rén ba
问 别 人 吧。

雪梅： Xuě méi　Qǐng wèn　zhè fù jìn yǒu méi yǒu yóu jú
雪梅：请问，这附近有没有邮局？

路人： Lù rén　Yóu jú
路人：邮局？

雪梅： Xuě méi　Jiù zhè jiā yóu jú
雪梅：就这家邮局。

路人： Lù rén　Zhè ge ya　nà nǐ men zǒu guò le　nǐ men děi shùn
路人：这个呀，那你们走过了，你们得顺
zhe zhè tiáo lù wǎng huí zǒu
着这条路往回走。

雪梅： Xuě méi　Xiè xie
雪梅：谢谢！

小杰： Xiǎo jié　Gǎn qing zǒu guò le　Mā ma wǒ kě zhēn è le　yào
小杰：敢情走过了。妈妈我可真饿了，要
bù wǒ men xiān tián bǎo dù zi hǎo bù hǎo
不我们先填饱肚子好不好？

雪梅： Xuě méi　Yǎn kàn jiù dào le　chī shén me fàn　Zài jiān chí
雪梅：眼看就到了，吃什么饭。再坚持
yí huìr
一会儿。

小杰： Xiǎo jié　Wǒ jiě jie kě zhēn xíng　zhè me dà gèr　lǐ bian
小杰：我姐姐可真行，这么大个儿，里边
dōu zhuāng le xiē shén me dōng xi a　Wǒ zhēn hèn
都装了些什么东西啊？我真恨
bu de mǎ shàng dǎ kāi kàn kan
不得马上打开看看。

雪梅： Xuě méi　Zhēn chén a　gòu zán men ná de
雪梅：真沉啊，够咱们拿的。

小杰： Xiǎo jié　Mā ma wǒ men xiàn zài wǎng nǎ biān zǒu
小杰：妈妈我们现在往哪边走？

雪梅： Xuě méi　Gāng cái wǒ men shì cóng nǎ biān guò lái de
雪梅：刚才我们是从哪边过来的？

Xiaojie: Mum, you are back.

Xuemei: Your sister has mailed us a parcel.

Xiaojie: Really? What is it? Have you got it?

Xuemei: I don't know. I haven't gone for it yet.

Xiaojie: How about going there now? It happens I am free. We can go together.

Xuemei: All right. But let me check the map and find out where the post office is first.

Xiaojie: It can't be that complicated with me here.

Xuemei: Stop boasting. OK. Let's go. We'll turn left at the door.

Xiaojie: Will we get there by walking straight ahead?

Xuemei: Turn at the third crossing.

Xiaojie: This is the third crossing.

Xuemei: Then turn right now and we'll get to the place soon.

Xiaojie: Mum, we've come a long way. Where is the post office?

Xuemei: I'm puzzled too. We should have found it by now. Come and look at the map.

Xiaojie: This map is too complicated. I bct even Chinese have problems following it. Let's go and ask someone for help.

Xuemei: Excuse me, is there a post office around here?

Passerby: Post office?

Xuemei: Is the post office here?

Passerby: Oh, this one. You've passed it. You should walk back along this road.

Xuemei: Thanks.

Xiaojie: We've already passed it. Mum, I'm really hungry. Can we try and get something to eat first?

Xuemei: We'll be there in a minute. Why eat now? Put up with it for a while.

Xiaojie: My sister is really great. It's such a big parcel. What's in it? I can't wait to open it.

Xuemei: It's so heavy. We can hardly carry it.

Xiaojie: Mum, which direction should we take now?

Xuemei: Which way did we come?

生词

1.	姐姐	jiě jie	名	elder sister
2.	包裹	bāo guǒ	名	parcel
3.	正好	zhèng hǎo	副	it just so happens
4.	地图	dì tú	名	map
5.	位置	wèi zhi	名	location
6.	吹牛	chuī niú	动	boast
7.	出发	chū fā	动	start out
8.	拐弯	guǎi wān	动	turn
9.	影	yǐng	名	trace
10.	纳闷	nà mèn	动	be puzzled
11.	按说	àn shuō	副	normally
12.	即使……也……	jí shǐ…yě…	副	even if
13.	恐怕	kǒng pà	副	be afraid, probably
14.	眼看	yǎn kàn	副	soon
15.	坚持	jiān chí	动	keep, persist
16.	恨不得	hèn bu de		be dying to

注释

1. 正好我也没事儿。
↪ It just happens that I'm not busy with anything. 正好 indicates a convenient coincidence, it just so happens.

2. 不至于那么复杂吧。
↪ It can't be that complicated. 不至于 means it can't be to such and such an extent.

3. 怎么还没看见邮局的影儿呢？
↪ How come there is still no trace of the post office? 影儿 means 影子, shadow. Here it's used to indicate a trace or a sign. They haven't seen any indication that the post office is near.

4. 我也有点儿纳闷儿。
↪ I'm a little confused too. 纳闷儿 is to be puzzled, to be bewildered.

5. 即使是中国人恐怕也看不懂。
↪ Even Chinese people would have trouble understanding it. Today we're going to do some practices with this pattern "即使 sth. 也", even or even if. 恐怕, as we learned earlier, indicates an estimate or a guess.

6. 你们得顺着这条路往回走。
↪ You have to follow this road back that way. 往回走 is to go back the way you came. 顺着, to follow.

7. 敢情走过了。
↪ It seems we've gone too far. 敢情 is a colloquial expression to indicate you've just discovered or just realized something.

8. 我真恨不得马上打开看看。
↪ I wish we could open it right away. 恨不得 means you wish for something, or to use more emphasis, you're dying to do something.

9. 真沉啊，够咱们拿的。
↪ 真沉啊, it's very heavy. 够咱们拿的, it's a real handful, it's enough for us to carry.

1. 正好 a convenient coincidence

我正好也要去那儿，明天咱们一起走吧。

It just happens that I'm going there as well. Let's go together tomorrow.

这件衣服我穿着正好合适。

When I wear this article of clothing, it's just right.

2. 恐怕 an estimate

我恐怕星期天不能去你家了。

I'm afraid I can't go to your house on Sunday.

他恐怕走了有二十天了。

I think he's been gone for roughly twenty days.

3. 恨不得 anxiously hoping for something

他恨不得能去每一个国家旅游。

He really hopes to travel to every country.

他恨不得一天就学完所有的课文。

He's so anxious. He wants to study all of the lessons in one day.

句型 及 替换练习

即使……，也…… even if/though

即使你说错了，也不要紧。

Even if you make a mistake, it's not important.

替换例句：

即使是冬天，他也坚持每天游泳。

即使我今天没时间去找你，我明天也一定会去。

第 5 课

交通事故
Traffic Accident

课文

男同事：小李啊，你今天报道写得真不错。
Nán tóng shì Xiǎo Lǐ a nǐ jīn tiān bào dào xiě de zhēn bú cuò

女同事：雪梅那篇写得也不错。雪梅今天怎么没来上班呢？
Nǚ tóng shì Xuě méi nà piān xiě de yě bú cuò Xuě méi jīn tiān zěn me méi lái shàng bān ne

男同事：她被车撞伤了，在家休息呢。
Nán tóng shì Tā bèi chē zhuàng shāng le zài jiā xiū xi ne

女同事：啊？真的，伤得重吗？
Nǚ tóng shì A Zhēn de shāng de zhòng ma

男同事：她给我打过电话。她在电话里说只是腿和胳膊受了一些伤。
Nán tóng shì Tā gěi wǒ dǎ guo diàn huà Tā zài diàn huà li shuō zhǐ shì tuǐ hé gē bo shòu le yì xiē shāng

女同事：那咱们一起去看看她吧。

男同事：好，我们先去买束鲜花吧。

男同事：雪梅，你好！

女同事

雪梅：你们好！请坐！鲜花真漂亮，谢谢你们来看我。

男同事：不用谢。雪梅，你好些了吗？

雪梅：我已经好多了。

女同事：怎么回事儿啊？

雪梅：别提了，我刚从书店出来，就被一辆车撞倒了。

女同事：那个司机开车也太不小心了吧。

男同事：唉，现在啊，马路上的"二把刀"太多了。

雪梅：也不全怪他，我光顾着看刚买的新书了，根本没注意到有车。

男同事：现在路上的汽车太多了，不论骑车还是走路，你都得小心。

雪梅：我当时也是稀里糊涂的，不知怎么地就被撞倒了。

男同事：真可怕，当时谁把你送到医院的？

雪梅：旁边一个过路的人，见我摔倒了，就打了120，叫了救护车。

女同事：那个司机呢？

雪梅：当时，他看见我流了那么多的血，都吓傻了。

男同事：那你的伤得多长时间才能好啊？

雪梅：还好，医生说骨头没事，我猜顶多两三个礼拜就没事了。

男同事：真是不幸中的万幸，那你也趁这个机会好好休息休息吧。

女同事：对，一定要多注意休息，工作上的事你就别操心了。

雪梅：事已至此，也没有别的办法了，只能
这么想了。

男同事：时间不早了。

女同事：是啊，雪梅，我们也该告辞了。

男同事：祝你早日康复！

雪梅：谢谢！

Male Colleague:	Xiao Li, your report today was well done.
Female Colleague:	Xuemei also did a good job. Why is Xuemei absent today?
Male Colleague:	She was hit by a car and is in hospital.
Female Colleague:	What? Really, is it serious?
Male Colleague:	She called me and told me that only her arms and legs were hurt.
Female Colleague:	Then let's go and visit her.
Male Colleague:	OK, let's go and get a bunch of flowers first.

Male Colleague Female Colleague:	Hello, Xuemei.
Xuemei:	Hello. Have a seat please. The flowers are beautiful. Thanks for coming visiting me.
Male Colleague:	You're welcome. Xuemei, are you feeling better now?
Xuemei:	I'm much better now.
Female Colleague:	What happened then?
Xuemei:	Hey, let's not talk about it. I was knocked over by a car as soon as I walked out of the bookstore.
Female Colleague:	That driver wasn't careful enough.

Male Colleague: Hey, there are too many bad drivers on the road these days.

Xuemei: You can't blame him entirely. I was absorbed in reading the book I'd just bought and didn't really pay any attention to the car.

Male Colleague: There are too many cars on the road. You have to be careful, whether you're cycling or walking.

Xuemei: I was absent-minded and got myself knocked over.

Male Colleague: Terrible. Who brought you to the hospital?

Xuemei: It was a passerby. He saw me on the ground and called 120 for an ambulance.

Female Colleague: What about that driver?

Xuemei: He saw I was bleeding badly and was frightened silly.

Male Colleague: When will you be fully recovered?

Xuemei: Not too long. The doctor said there's no bone damage. And I guess I'll be fine in at most two or three weeks.

Male Colleague: That's something good to know among all the misfortune. And you can take advantage of the opportunity to take a good rest.

Female Colleague: Right, be sure to take enough rest. Don't worry about your work.

Xuemei: What's done is done. There is nothing I can do about it now. That's how I must think.

Male Colleague: It's late.

Female Colleague: Yes. We'll leave now.

Male Colleague: Get well soon!

Xuemei: Thanks.

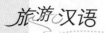

1.	报道	bào dào	名	report
2.	撞	zhuàng	动	hit
3.	腿	tuǐ	名	leg
4.	胳膊	gē bo	名	arm
5.	束	shù	量	bunch
6.	鲜花	xiān huā	名	fresh flowers
7.	根本	gēn běn	副	at all
8.	稀里糊涂	xī li hú tú		muddle-headed
9.	可怕	kě pà	形	terrible
10.	医院	yī yuàn	名	hospital
11.	救护车	jiù hù chē	名	ambulance
12.	流血	liú xiě	动	bleed
13.	医生	yī shēng	名	doctor
14.	骨头	gǔ tou	名	bone
15.	礼拜	lǐ bài	名	week
16.	机会	jī huì	名	opportunity
17.	操心	cāo xīn	动	worry about
18.	告辞	gào cí	动	take leave
19.	早日	zǎo rì	副	soon
20.	康复	kāng fù	动	get well, recover

注释

1．她被车撞伤了。

⊃ She's been hit and injured by a car. 撞 is to crash into something. 伤 is an injury.

2．（她）只是腿和胳膊受了一些伤。

⊃ Only her leg and arm have been hurt. 只是 indicates that it is not as serious as you might expect or fear.

3．别提了。

⊃ Literally this means don't mention it, it's more like "don't remind me, I don't want to talk about it", or perhaps " it's difficult to talk about it".

4．马路上的"二把刀"太多了。

⊃ There are too many bad drivers on the road. 一把手 is a phrase used to describe No.1, an expert, the best. 二把刀 is a similar expression, but this time it refers to an amateur, or someone who just barely knows what he's doing. Translating 二把刀 as "bad driver" doesn't necessarily give the proper feeling to this term. Something like "bonehead" would be more appropriate.

5．也不全怪他，我光顾着看刚买的新书了。

⊃ 也不全怪他, it's not all his fault. 怪 is to blame somebody.

6．我当时也是稀里糊涂的。

⊃ I was totally confused. You can't afford to be 稀里糊涂. This is a set phrase. 糊涂 is to be confused. 稀里糊涂 really just means the same thing, but is more colloquial and slightly more exaggerated.

7．旁边一个过路的人，见我摔倒了，就打了120，叫了救护车。

⊃ Here 就 indicates that something happened very quickly thereafter.

8．都吓傻了。

⊃ 吓傻了 is literally to be stupefied, you're so scared you don't know what to do.

9．我猜顶多两三个礼拜就没事了。

⊃ I guess I'll be OK in 2 or 3 weeks at most. 顶多 is at maximum, at most. You could substitute this for 最多.

10．事已至此，也没有别的办法了。

⊃ The situation has already come to this point, what's done is done. 事已至此, this is a somewhat classical expression. 至 is to arrive, to come to.

11．我们也该告辞了。

⊃ We'll leave now. 告辞 is like the English expression "to take our leave". It's just a fancy or more classical way of saying goodbye.

文化
背景

Traffic Safety

There are three emergency numbers you should remember when you are traveling in China. 110 is for police, 119 is for the fire department and 120 for an ambulance. In North America and other countries, the equivalent number would be 911.

China is a kingdom of bicycles. There are more bikes produced, exported, bought domestically and ridden in China than anywhere else in the world.

Unlike in North America, roads in Beijing were largely designed with bicycles in mind. After all, it wasn't that long ago that the bicycle was the most common form of transportation in Beijing. So there were large bicycle lanes that were separated from cars, and many bridges even had double layers, so that bicycles and cars could keep separate from each other.

With the huge boom in domestic car production and sales these past few years, traffic has become much more complicated. New expressways have been built just for cars, where bicycles and pedestrians are strictly forbidden. Other times, what used to be a very wide lane for bicycles has now been divided into one car lane and one smaller bicycle lane. With all the intersections and turn-offs, the two types of vehicles still have a lot of opportunity to meet. Unfortunately, if you're riding a bike, you may legally have the right of way, but it's always best to ride defensively and be careful.

只是 only，just

我只是随便看看，不打算买什么。

I'm just looking around. I don't plan on buying anything.

他一句话也不说，只是静静地坐在那儿。

He didn't say anything. He just sat there quietly.

句型 及 替换 练习

不论……，都…… no matter what situation or condition

不论是刮风还是下雨，他都坚持跑步。

No matter whether it's windy or it's raining, he insists on running.

替换例句：

不论是打篮球不是打排球，他都很拿手。

不论是老人还是孩子，都喜欢听他的歌。

第 *6* 课

香山
Fragrant Hills

课文

Xiǎo jié
小 杰：这 里 的 风 景 真 好，就 像 世 外 什
me lái zhe
么 来 着？

Biǎo jiě
表 姐：就 像 世 外 桃 源 一 样。

Xiǎo jié
小 杰：对 对 对，老 师 刚 教 的。哎，姑 姑，
wǒ gāng cái kàn jiàn nà bian yǒu hěn duō lǎo rén zài
我 刚 才 看 见 那 边 有 很 多 老 人 在
yùn dòng
运 动。

Biǎo jiě
表 姐：可 不 是，老 年 人 比 年 轻 人 更 热 衷

yú duàn liàn shēn tǐ　　Zhèr fēng jǐng yòu měi　　kōng
于 锻 炼 身 体 。 这 儿 风 景 又 美 ， 空

qì yòu hǎo　　shì gè duàn liàn de hǎo dì fang
气 又 好 ， 是 个 锻 炼 的 好 地 方 。

Xiǎo jié　　Wǒ tīng bà ba shuō qiū tiān de Xiāng shān zuì měi
小 杰 ： 我 听 爸 爸 说 秋 天 的 香 山 最 美 。

Biǎo jiě　　Qí shí Xiāng shān yì nián sì jì dōu bú cuò　　Dōng
表 姐 ： 其 实 香 山 一 年 四 季 都 不 错 。 冬

tiān xià le xuě jiù gèng piào liang le　　Xī shān qíng xuě
天 下 了 雪 就 更 漂 亮 了 ，"西 山 晴 雪"

hái shì gè yǒu míng de jǐng guān ne
还 是 个 有 名 的 景 观 呢 。

Xiǎo jié　　Shì ma　　wǒ dōu děng bù jí la　　Dào shí hou　　nín
小 杰 ： 是 吗 ， 我 都 等 不 及 啦 。 到 时 候 ， 您

yí dìng yào dài wǒ lái kàn kan
一 定 要 带 我 来 看 看 。

Biǎo jiě　　Méi wèn tí　　bǎo zhèng ràng nǐ yì bǎo yǎn fú
表 姐 ： 没 问 题 ， 保 证 让 你 一 饱 眼 福 。

Xiǎo jié　　Tài hǎo la　　Gū gu　　zán men jīn tiān yì qǐ pá
小 杰 ： 太 好 啦 ！ 姑 姑 ， 咱 们 今 天 一 起 爬

shàng qù zěn me yàng
上 去 怎 么 样 ？

Biǎo jiě　　Hǎo　　nà jiù pá shàng qù　　nán dé yí gè duàn liàn
表 姐 ： 好 ， 那 就 爬 上 去 ， 难 得 一 个 锻 炼

shēn tǐ de hǎo jī hui
身 体 的 好 机 会 。

Xiǎo jié　　Kuài diǎnr　　kuài diǎnr　　Nín tài màn la　　wǒ zài
小 杰 ： 快 点 儿 ， 快 点 儿 ！ 您 太 慢 啦 ， 我 在

shàng miàn děng nín ba　　Ai yao
上 面 等 您 吧 。 哎 唷 ！

Biǎo jiě　　Zěn me le　　Xiǎo jié　　Kuài ràng wǒ kàn kan
表 姐 ： 怎 么 了 ， 小 杰 ？ 快 让 我 看 看 。

Xiǎo jié　Hǎo xiàng wǒ de jiǎo　　wǎi le
小杰：好像我的脚……崴了。

Biǎo jié　Nǐ xiān màn man zhàn qǐ lai　kàn kan néng bù néng
表姐：你先慢慢站起来，看看能不能。

Xiǎo jié　O　bù xíng bù xíng　tài téng le
小杰：哦，不行不行，太疼了。

Biǎo jié　Nà néng dòng ma
表姐：那能动吗？

Xiǎo jié　Bù　hǎo xiàng zhè zhī jiǎo bù gǎn zhān dì
小杰：不，好像这只脚不敢沾地。

Biǎo jié　Nǐ xiān zuò huìr　wǒ gěi jí jiù zhōng xīn dǎ gè
表姐：你先坐会儿，我给急救中心打个
diàn huà
电话。

Biǎo jié　Hǎo de　hǎo de　xiè xie nín　Xiǎo jié　yī shēng
表姐：好的，好的，谢谢您。小杰，医生
mǎ shàng jiù dào le　Wǒ kàn kan nǐ de jiǎo　āi
马上就到了。我看看你的脚，哎
ya　dōu zhǒng le　wǎn shang kěn dìng huì zhǒng de
呀，都肿了，晚上肯定会肿得
gèng lì hai
更厉害。

Xiǎo jié　Wǒ xiàn zài jué de yuè lái yuè téng le
小杰：我现在觉得越来越疼了。

Biǎo jié　Xiǎo jié　yī shēng lái la
表姐：小杰，医生来啦！

Yī shēng　Nín hǎo　Zěn me yàng　Shāng de zhòng bú zhòng
医生：您好。怎么样？伤得重不重？

Biǎo jié　Nín kàn kan ba　tā de jiǎo wǎi le
表姐：您看看吧，她的脚崴了。

Yī shēng　Bié zháo jí　ràng wǒ jiǎn chá yí xià
医生：别着急，让我检查一下。

Yī shēng　Jiù mù qián de qíng kuàng kàn　wèn tí bú dà　wǒ
医生：就目前的情况看，问题不大，我

xiān gěi tā chǔ lǐ yí xià
先 给 她 处 理 一 下 。

Biǎo jiě　Nà yí huìr　tā néng zì jǐ zǒu ma
表 姐：那 一 会 儿 她 能 自 己 走 吗？

Yī shēng　Kǒng pà bù xíng　Jí biàn méi yǒu duō dà de wèn tí
医 生：恐 怕 不 行。即 便 没 有 多 大 的 问 题，

nǐ men yě děi xiān qù tàng yī yuàn jiǎn chá yí xiàr
你 们 也 得 先 去 趟 医 院 检 查 一 下 儿。

Xiǎo jié　Gū gu　wǒ bì xū qù yī yuàn ma　Wǒ jué de wǒ
小 杰：姑 姑，我 必 须 去 医 院 吗？我 觉 得 我

néng zǒu
能 走。

Yī shēng　Nǐ xiàn zài de qíng kuàng　bù jǐn bù néng zǒu lù
医 生：你 现 在 的 情 况，不 仅 不 能 走 路，

ér qiě hái yào bì miǎn cháng shí jiān de zhàn lì
而 且 还 要 避 免 长 时 间 的 站 立。

Biǎo jiě　Nǐ hái shi tīng yī shēng de huà　hǎo hǎo pèi hé yī
表 姐：你 还 是 听 医 生 的 话，好 好 配 合 医

shēng zhì liáo ba
生 治 疗 吧。

Xiǎo jié　Nà hǎo ba
小 杰：那 好 吧。

Yī shēng　Jí jiù chē jiù zài shān xià　Wǒ xiàn zài jiào gōng zuò
医 生：急 救 车 就 在 山 下。我 现 在 叫 工 作

rén yuán bǎ dān jià tái shàng lái
人 员 把 担 架 抬 上 来。

Biǎo jiě　Tài hǎo le　xiè xie nín
表 姐：太 好 了，谢 谢 您。

Yī shēng　Bú kè qi
医 生：不 客 气。

Biǎo jiě　Xiǎo jié　yǐ hòu pá shān kě yào xiǎo xīn
表 姐：小 杰，以 后 爬 山 可 要 小 心！

Xiaojie: The scenery here is really beautiful. It's like Xana...en...

Cousin: It's like Xanadu.

Xiaojie: Right, I just learned that in class. Hey, aunt, I see there are many senior citizens doing exercises in the park.

Cousin: Old people are more serious about exercising than the young, aren't they? What's more, the scenery is beautiful and the air here is fresh. It is a good place for exercising.

Xiaojie: My father told me that the Fragrant Hills are most beautiful in autumn.

Cousin: Actually the Fragrant Hills are beautiful all year round. Even more so in winter with the snow. Besides, "Snow on the Western Hills on a sunny day" is a famous scene.

Xiaojie: Really, I can't wait. You absolutely must bring me here then.

Cousin: No problem, you're really in for a sight.

Xiaojie: Terrific. Aunt, how about we climb up to the top together today?

Cousin: OK, let's climb together. This is really a rare opportunity to do some exercise.

Xiaojie: Aunt, hurry. You're too slow. I'll see you at the top. Ouch!

Cousin: What's wrong with you, Xiaojie? Let me check.

Xiaojie: I've sprained my ankle.

Cousin: Can you try to move?

Xiaojie: Ouch, no, no. It hurts.

Cousin: Try to move it a bit.

Xiaojie: I can't even touch the ground with this foot.

Cousin: You sit here and I'll call the emergency centre.

Cousin: OK, thank you! Xiaojie, the doctor will be here soon. Look at your foot. It's swollen. I'm sure it will get more serious in the evening.

Xiaojie: Aunt, it's hurting even more.

Cousin: Xiaojie, here comes the doctor.

Doctor: Hello. What's wrong? Is it serious?

Cousin: Doctor, she's sprained her ankle. Please examine her.

Doctor: Don't worry. Let me check.

Doctor: So far, it doesn't look too serious. I'll give it some treatment.

Cousin: Can she walk by herself ?

Doctor: I'm afraid not. You should go to the hospital first. Go and have it examined at the hospital even if it isn't serious.

Xiaojie: Aunt, do I have to go to the hospital? I think I can walk.

Doctor: In your condition, you can't walk and should avoid standing for too long.

Cousin: You should take the doctor's advice and be cooperative.

Xiaojie: OK.

Doctor: The ambulance is down the hill. I'll send staff for a stretcher.

Cousin: Wonderful, thank you very much.

Doctor: You are welcome.

Cousin: Xiaojie, be careful when climbing a hill in the future.

1.	世外桃源	shì wài táo yuán	名	Xanadu
2.	运动	yùn dòng	动	do exercise
3.	热衷	rè zhōng	动	be keen on
4.	锻炼	duàn liàn	动	do physical exercise
5.	空气	kōng qì	名	air
6.	香山	Xiāng shān	名	the Fragrant Hills
7.	四季	sì jì	名	four seasons
8.	景观	jǐng guān	名	sight
9.	等不及	děng bu jí		can't wait
10.	保证	bǎo zhèng	动	guarantee, promise
11.	一饱眼福	yì bǎo yǎn fú		feast one's eyes on something
12.	难得	nán dé	副	rarely
13.	崴	wǎi	动	sprain
14.	急救中心	jí jiù zhōng xīn	名	first aid center
15.	肿	zhǒng	形	swollen
16.	目前	mù qián	名	present time
17.	情况	qíng kuàng	名	circumstance
18.	处理	chǔ lǐ	动	handle
19.	避免	bì miǎn	动	avoid
20.	配合	pèi hé	动	cooperate
21.	治疗	zhì liáo	动	cure
22.	急救车	jí jiù chē	名	ambulance
23.	担架	dān jià	名	stretcher

注释

1. 就像世外桃源一样。
- The phrase 世外桃源 comes from classical literature, *The Story of the Peach Blossom Valley*. 世外桃源 is Shangri-la, a perfect imaginary world.

2. 老年人比年轻人更热衷于锻炼身体。这儿风景又美，空气又好，是个锻炼的好地方。
- 热衷 is to love something, or to be devoted to it. Here, the pattern "又 sth. 又 sth. else" is used to list two reasons why there are so many people.

3. 没问题，保证让你一饱眼福。
- 福 is blessing or good fortune. 饱 is to be full. Your eyes will be full of blessings. In other words, you'll be dazzled.

4. 难得一个锻炼身体的好机会。
- This is a rare opportunity to get some good exercises. 难得 indicates that something is rare. 难得的机会, a rare opportunity.

5. 脚崴了
- 崴 is to twist or to sprain. This is a verb specifically used to refer to feet or ankles.

6. 这只脚不敢沾地。
- I can't walk on this foot. Here, 沾 literally means to touch.

7. 就目前的情况看，问题不大。
- As far as it looks now, it's not a big problem. 目前 is like 现在, and it literally means right in front of your eyes, now.

8. 不仅不能走路，而且还要避免长时间的站立。
- Here's another useful pattern " 不仅 sth. 也...", not only, but also. Not only can you not walk, but you should also avoid standing for long periods of time.

9. 你还是听医生的话，好好配合医生治疗吧。
- It's always a good idea to listen to the doctor. 配合 is to cooperate. 治疗, treatment.

10. 我现在叫工作人员把担架抬上来。
- 抬 is to carry with both hands. 抬担架, to carry a stretcher.

Fragrant Hills

The Western Hills of Beijing are a popular recreation destination. Because of the relative coolness in summer, this area has always been used as a retreat by high officials. The most popular area of the hills is 香山, the Fragrant Hills, located just west of the Summer Palace. This area is most famous for the dramatic red colours of the fall, but as was explained in the dialogue, there is something you can see here all the year round. A cable car will take you to the top of the hill if you're not interested in the exercise.

While near the Fragrant Hills, you might want to visit 碧云寺, the Azure Clouds Temple. With its striking dagoba and stupas, it has a rather Indian feel to it. This is also the place where Sun Yat-sen, the founder of the Republic of China in 1911, was briefly interred after he died before his eventual resting place, the Zhong Shan Mausoleum near Nanjing, was completed.

One important detail to note is that at many tourist destinations, accident insurance is often included with the ticket. In the case of Xiaojie's accident today, she should be covered by this insurance. Of course, it's always best to have your own comprehensive insurance coverage.

语言
点

1. 热衷 to be devoted to something

他十分热衷于滑冰。

He's really devoted to skating.

2. 难得 a rare occurrence

这次来中国工作是一个难得的机会。

This is a rare opportunity to come to China and work.

3. 肯定 surely

你肯定没来过这个地方。

You surely have never been here before.

句型 及 替换练习

即便……，也…… even though

即便现在不堵车，你也得提前一个小时出发。

Even though there's no traffic jam, you should leave an hour in advance.

替换例句：

即便你现在不告诉我，我也会想办法打听出来的。

即便现在不堵车，你也得提前一点儿出发。

第 7 课

生病
Get Sick

课文

Biǎo jiě　Nín hǎo　wǒ men xiǎng guà gè nèi kē hào　qǐng
表姐：您好，我们想挂个内科号，请

wèn shì zài nín zhèr　guà ma
问是在您这儿挂吗？

Hù shi　Bù　wǒ men　zhèr　bù xū yào guà hào　Qǐng
护士：不，我们这儿不需要挂号。请

wèn nín shì dì yī cì lái zhèr　ma
问您是第一次来这儿吗？

Biǎo jiě　Shì de
表姐：是的。

Hù shi　Xīn bìng rén xū yào zhù cè yí xiàr　má fan tián yí
护士：新病人需要注册一下儿，麻烦填一

xià biǎo gé
下表格。

护士： Hù shi
您看的是内科。内科在对面那个楼，
Nín kàn de shì nèi kē Nèi kē zài duì miàn nà ge lóu
二层。
èr céng

护士： Hù shi
您好，请问您哪儿不舒服？
Nín hǎo qǐng wèn nín nǎr bù shū fu

雪梅： Xuě méi
我一直咳嗽。
Wǒ yì zhí ké sou

护士： Hù shi
发烧吗？如果发烧，需要先试表，
Fā shāo ma Rú guǒ fā shāo xū yào xiān shì biǎo
量量体温。
liáng liang tǐ wēn

雪梅： Xuě méi
不，不发烧，我自己在家里刚量过。
Bù bù fā shāo wǒ zì jǐ zài jiā li gāng liáng guò

护士： Hù shi
那您稍等一下儿，我看医生有没
Nà nín shāo děng yí xiàr wǒ kàn yī shēng yǒu méi
有时间。
yǒu shí jiān

表姐： Biǎo jiě
今天病人挺多的，不过好在诊室
Jīn tiān bìng rén tǐng duō de bú guò hǎo zài zhěn shì
多，要不然不知道得等到什么
duō yào bù rán bù zhī dào děi děng dào shén me
时候呢！
shí hou ne

护士： Hù shi
雪梅，到你了。
Xuě méi dào nǐ le

雪梅： Xuě méi
谢谢！
Xiè xie

表姐： Biǎo jiě
那我在这儿等你。
Nà wǒ zài zhèr děng nǐ

Yī shēng　　Nín hǎo　　Zěn me le　　Zěn me bù shū fu
医　生：您好！怎么了？怎么不舒服？

Xuě méi　　Ké sou
雪　梅：咳嗽。

Yī shēng　　Ké jǐ tiān le
医　生：咳几天了？

Xuě méi　　Yí gè duō xīng qī le　　ér qiě yì ké qǐ lái jiù
雪　梅：一个多星期了，而且一咳起来就
　　　　　zhǐ bú zhù
　　　　　止不住。

Yī shēng　　Nà nǐ xiān qù zuò gè tòu shì
医　生：那你先去做个透视。

Xuě méi　　Dài fu ràng wǒ qù tòu shì
雪　梅：大夫让我去透视。

Biǎo jiě　　Nà děi xiān jiāo qián cái xíng　　Zǒu ba　　wǒ péi nǐ
表　姐：那得先交钱才行。走吧，我陪你
　　　　　yí kuàir qù
　　　　　一块儿去。

Xuě méi　　Dài fu　　zhè shì tòu shì de jié guǒ　　nín gěi kàn kan
雪　梅：大夫，这是透视的结果，您给看看。

Yī shēng　　Hǎo　　Bú yào jǐn　　méi shén me tài dà wèn tí
医　生：好！不要紧，没什么太大问题。

　　　　　Qǐng zuò　　wǒ gěi nǐ jiǎn chá yí xiàr　　Nín jué de
　　　　　请坐，我给你检查一下儿。您觉得
　　　　　sǎng zi zěn me yàng
　　　　　嗓子怎么样？

Xuě méi　　Sǎng zi bù shū fu　　bù guāng shì fā yǎng　　ér qiě
雪　梅：嗓子不舒服，不光是发痒，而且
　　　　　hěn téng
　　　　　很疼。

医　生：来，张开嘴让我看看。

医　生：嗓子红了，发炎了。我给你开点儿
药吧，你先吃几天看看，不好的
话再打针。

雪　梅：但愿吃了药就好了，我实在害
怕打针。

医　生：有没有过敏的药物？

雪　梅：没有。

医　生：我给你开三种药，这个药一天
三次，一次一片。另外两种都是
一天两次，饭后服用。

雪　梅：谢谢大夫。

医　生：回去以后还要注意保暖，多喝水。

雪　梅：好，谢谢您！

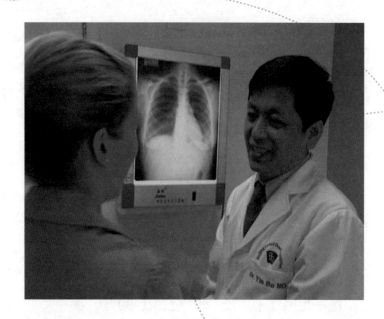

Cousin: Hello. We'd like to register for the clinical section. Is this the right place?

Nurse: There's normally no need to sign in here. Is this your first time?

Cousin: Yes, the first time.

Nurse: Then you need to register. Please fill out this form.

Nurse: You want to see the clinical section? It's on the second floor on the opposite building.

Nurse: Hello, what seems to be the problem?

Xuemei: I have a persistent cough.

Nurse: Do you have a fever? If you do, then we need to take your temperature first.

Xuemei: No, there is no fever. I've just taken my temperature myself at home.

Nurse: Then please wait and I'll go and see if the doctor has time now.

Cousin: There are a lot of patients today. It's just as well there are a lot of treatment rooms, otherwise who knows how long you'd have to wait!

Nurse: Xuemei, it's your turn.

Xuemei: Thanks.

Cousin: OK, I'll wait for you there.

Doctor: Hello. What's wrong? Where do you feel unwell?

Xuemei: I have a cough.

Doctor: How many days have you had it?

Xuemei: Over a week now, and once I start coughing I can't stop.

Doctor: Go and get an X-ray done first.

Xuemei: The doctor asked me to get an X-ray.

Cousin: You have to pay first. Come on, I'll come with you.

Xuemei: Doctor, this is the X-ray result. Please have a look.

Doctor: Don't worry. It's nothing serious. Sit down please. Let me
         check it for you. How's your throat?

Xuemei: My throat feels bad, not just itchy, but painful as well.

Doctor: Open your mouth and let me have a look.

Doctor: Your throat's red. There's inflammation. I'll write you a
         prescription for some medicine. If you still aren't better
         after a few days, then you'll need an injection.

Xuemei: I hope the medication's enough. I'm really scared of needles.

Doctor: Are you allergic to any medication?

Xuemei: No.

Doctor: I'll prescribe three types of medicine. This one you take
         three times daily, one tablet at a time. The other two are to
         be taken twice a day, after food.

Xuemei: Thanks.

Doctor: Don't forget to keep warm and drink lots of water.

Xuemei: Thank you, doctor!

 生词

1.	内科	nèi kē	名	internal medicine
2.	挂号	guà hào	动	register at hospital
3.	病人	bìng rén	名	patient
4.	注册	zhù cè	动	register
5.	咳嗽	ké sou	动	cough
6.	发烧	fā shāo	动	have a fever
7.	量	liáng	动	measure
8.	体温	tǐ wēn	名	body temperature
9.	诊室	zhěn shì	名	treatment room
10.	透视	tòu shì	名	X-ray
11.	嗓子	sǎng zi	名	throat
12.	不光······ 而且······	bù guāng…ér qiě…		not only…but also…
13.	发痒	fā yǎng	形	itchy
14.	发炎	fā yán	动	become inflamed
15.	打针	dǎ zhēn	动	have an injection
16.	但愿	dàn yuàn	副	if only
17.	害怕	hài pà	动	be afraid
18.	过敏	guò mǐn	动	be allergic to
19.	药物	yào wù	名	medicine
20.	保暖	bǎo nuǎn	动	keep warm

注释

1. 挂号

⟳ 挂号 is to register at the hospital. 我挂一个内科, I'd like to register for internal medicine. 内科 refers to medical treatment other than surgery, for instance, treating with medicines.

2. 发烧吗？如果发烧，需要先试表，量量体温。

⟳ If you suspect you have a fever, you should 试表, use a thermometer, 量量体温, check your body temperature.

3. 要不然不知道得等到什么时候呢！

⟳ Otherwise, who knows how long we would have to wait. With the 呢 ending in this sentence, 不知道 is more like "who knows" than "I don't know".

4. 一咳起来就止不住。

⟳ Once I start coughing I can't stop. 止咳 is to stop coughing. 止不住, to not be able to stop coughing.

5. 大夫让我去透视。

⟳ The doctor asked or told me to have an X-ray. 透视 literally means to see through. This is a term for an X-ray, which is called literally X光. 让 means to allow, but here it's used in the sense to tell, or to ask somebody to do something.

6. 不光是发痒，而且很疼。

⟳ Not only is it itchy or irritated, it also hurts a lot. 不光 sth. 而且, not only, but also.

7. 我给你开点儿药吧。

⟳ I'll write a prescription for you. 开药 is to write a prescription.

8. 我实在害怕打针。

⟳ I'm really afraid of having a needle. 实在 is really, in reality. Here it's just used for emphasis.

Seeing a Doctor in China

Hospitals in major cities in China are quite modern. Many of the larger hospitals will have special reception areas for foreign nationals where you can receive priority treatment, but at a higher cost. There are also private hospitals that have been set up by foreign investors in cities like Beijing and Shanghai. These offer the most modern treatment, often with foreign doctors and nurses. But these clinics and hospitals are also by far the most expensive option.

Chinese hospitals are organized into departments or 科. For example, paediatrics is 儿科, gynecology is 妇科, but you will also find departments called 内科 and 外科. 外科 is basically surgery, or any treatment for injury, deformity or disease by manual or instrumental means. 内科 is the opposite, the treatment of disease by internal means, like taking medicines.

When visiting a Chinese hospital, the first thing to do is 挂号, register. This literally means "to hang a number". In effect, you are given a number. The first question you may be asked is 挂什么号? What kind of number do you want to hang, in other words, what kind of department. Rather than just go to one reception, you might have to first find, for example, the paediatric ward first, if you are looking for a doctor who specializes in children's diseases. Then you may have to decide whether you want regular treatment or you want to see a senior specialist. If so, you need to 挂专家号, to see a specialist.

1. 好在 fortunately

我昨天丢了钱包，好在后来警察帮我找到了。

Yesterday, I lost my wallet. Fortunately, a police officer helped me find it later on.

好在路不算远，明天我再来一趟。

Fortunately, it's not very far away. I'll come again tomorrow.

2. 让 allow, let

是她让我来找你的。

She was the one who asked me to come and look for you.

门口的服务员不让我进去。

The salesperson at the door won't let me in.

3. 实在 really

下过雨以后，这里的路实在太难走了。

After it rains, the roads here are really too difficult to travel.

这里的东西实在是太便宜了。

The things here are really far too cheap.

句型 及 替换练习

不光……，而且…… not only... but also...

那家饭店不光环境好，而且菜的味道也很正宗。

That restaurant does not only have a beautiful environment, but also the dishes taste very authentic.

替换例句：

这里的衣服，不光款式新颖，而且价格也十分便宜。

她不光人长得漂亮，而且也十分聪明。

感冒
Catch Cold

课文

Xiǎo jié　　Mā ma
小 杰：妈 妈。

Xuě méi　　Huí lái le　　jīn tiān xué xiào zěn me·yàng
雪 梅：回 来 了，今 天 学 校 怎 么 样？

Xiǎo jié　　Wǒ yǒu diǎnr bù shū fu
小 杰：我 有 点儿 不 舒 服。

Xuě méi　　Nǎr bù shū fu　　wǒ kàn kan　　you　　hěn rè
雪 梅：哪儿 不 舒 服，我 看 看，哟，很 热。

Xiǎo jié　　Wǒ hún shēn yì diǎnr jìnr dōu méi yǒu
小 杰：我 浑 身 一 点儿 劲儿 都 没 有。

Xuě méi　　Wǒ gěi nǐ liàng yí xiàr tǐ wēn
雪 梅：我 给 你 量 一 下儿 体 温。

Xiǎo jié　　Wǒ men bān yǒu hěn duō tóng xué dōu gǎn mào le
小 杰：我 们 班 有 很 多 同 学 都 感 冒 了。

雪梅： Xuě méi　O shì ma　Sān shí qī dù bā　yǒu diǎnr gāo
哦，是吗？三十七度八，有点儿高。

Nǐ ké sou ma　bǎo bèi
你咳嗽吗，宝贝？

小杰： Xiǎo jié　Wǒ jī běn bù ké sou
我基本不咳嗽。

雪梅： Xuě méi　Kě néng shì gǎn mào le　ràng nǐ duō chuān diǎnr
可能是感冒了，让你多穿点儿

yī fu　nǐ piān bù tīng　Nǐ chī diǎnr yào ba
衣服，你偏不听。你吃点儿药吧。

雪梅： Xuě méi　Zāo gāo　jiā li de gǎn mào yào dōu bèi nǐ bà ba dài
糟糕，家里的感冒药都被你爸爸带

zǒu le
走了。

小杰： Xiǎo jié　Wǒ bù xiǎng chī yào　zhǐ xiǎng shuì jiào
我不想吃药，只想睡觉。

雪梅： Xuě méi　Zhè jǐ tiān jiàng wēn le　bié shuō nǐ yí gè xiǎo hái
这几天降温了，别说你一个小孩

zi　lián dà ren yě yǒu hěn duō gǎn mào de
子，连大人也有很多感冒的。

小杰： Xiǎo jié　Mā ma　nǐ bié dān xīn　wǒ shuì yí huìr jiù
妈妈，你别担心，我睡一会儿就

hǎo le
好了。

雪梅： Xuě méi　Wǒ xiàn zài jiù qù mǎi yào　nǐ hē diǎnr rè shuǐ
我现在就去买药，你喝点儿热水，

chū diǎnr hàn　wǒ mǎ shàng huí lái
出点儿汗，我马上回来。

卖药人： Mài yào rén　Nín hǎo　nín yào shén me yào
您好，您要什么药？

雪梅： Xuě méi　Wǒ xiǎng mǎi diǎnr gǎn mào yào
我想买点儿感冒药。

卖药人：这几种都是感冒药，您要哪一种？

雪梅：我女儿浑身没劲儿、发烧，还有点儿咳嗽，您看哪种好呢？

卖药人：那您看这种怎么样？

雪梅：这还比较对症。这是中药还是西药？

卖药人：这是中药，它的副作用比西药小。

雪梅：一盒能吃几天？

卖药人：一天两次，一盒能吃五天。

雪梅：那我买两盒吧，这药的保质期是多长时间呢？

卖药人：生产日期在这儿，您看看。这药卖得快着呢，这都是新来的药。

雪梅：好的，谢谢。在哪儿交钱呢？

卖药人：那边儿。

Xiaojie: Mum.

Xuemei: You're back. How was school today?

Xiaojie: Mum, I don't feel well.

Xuemei: What's wrong? Let me see. Oh, you're very hot.

Xiaojie: I feel weak all over.

Xuemei: I'll take your temperature.

Xiaojie: A lot of kids in my class have caught colds.

Xuemei: Really? 37.8 degrees, a little high. Do you have a cough, dear?

Xiaojie: Not really.

Xuemei: Maybe you've caught a cold. I told you to dress more warmly. You never listen. Take some medicine.

Xuemei: Oh no, your dad's taken all the cold medicine with him.

Xiaojie: I don't want to take any medicine. I just want to sleep.

Xuemei: There's been a cold front in the last few days. Adults are catching colds, not to mention kids.

Xiaojie: Mum, don't worry. I just need to sleep for a while.

Xuemei: I'll go and buy some medicine now. You drink some hot water to sweat a little bit. I will be back soon.

Pharmacist: Hello. What can I do for you?

Xuemei: I'd like some cold medicine.

Pharmacist: These are all for colds. Which kind do you want?

Xuemei: My daughter feels weak all over, high temperature, a bit of a cough. Which medicine is the best?

Pharmacist: How about this one?

Xuemei: This is the right one. Is it tcaditional Chinese or western medicine?

Pharmacist: Chinese. It has fewer side effects than western medicine.

Xuemei: How long will a box last?

Pharmacist: Twice a day, it's enough for five days.

Xuemei: I'll take two boxes. How long does this medicine keep effective?

Pharmacist: Here's the production date. Look, this medicine is selling really fast. These are all new.

Xuemei: OK, thank you. Where do I pay?

Pharmacist: Over there.

生词

1.	浑身	hún shēn	名	the whole body
2.	劲儿	jìnr	名	strength
3.	感冒	gǎn mào	动	catch cold
4.	基本	jī běn	副	basically
5.	偏	piān	副	insistently
6.	糟糕	zāo gāo	形	bad
7.	降温	jiàng wēn	动	drop in temperature
8.	对症	duì zhèng	动	be the right cure
9.	中药	Zhōng yào	名	traditional Chinese medicine
10.	西药	Xī yào	名	western medicine
11.	副作用	fù zuò yòng	名	side effect
12.	盒	hé	量	box
13.	保质期	bǎo zhì qī	名	expiry period, shelf life
14.	生产	shēng chǎn	动	produce
15.	日期	rì qī	名	date

注释

1. 我浑身一点儿劲儿都没有。
- Literally, I have no strength or energy anywhere in my body.

2. 让你多穿点儿衣服，你偏不听。
- I told you to wear more clothing, but you didn't listen. Today we're going to learn about 偏, to indicate that an action has been done deliberately against someone's wishes.

3. 别说你一个小孩子，连大人也有很多感冒的。
- Not only children, many adults have also caught colds. "别说 sth. 连 sth. else" is like saying "not to mention sth., but also sth. else".

4. 我睡一会儿就好了。
- I'll be OK after sleeping for a while.

5. 保质期
- Here we see two similar terms. 保质期, expiry period, how long the product will be effective, and 生产日期, the production date. Usually, Chinese products list the production date and the length of time it can be stored, rather than just listing the actual expiry date.

Chinese Medicine

Traditional Chinese medicines are still widely available in China. Many people consider them better than Western medicines for minor illnesses like colds and the flu, but you will commonly find both types available in Chinese drugstores.

中药 is the term commonly used for traditional Chinese medicines, to distinguish them from 西药, Western medicines. Since traditional Chinese medicines are often made from herbs and other plants, they are also often called 草药 or 中草药. There are many other strange ingredients, from deer horn to snake gall bladder.

Sometimes these medicines are now refined, processed and manufactured into pills, dissolvable pouches and other modern forms. In traditional medicine stores, they can often mix the natural ingredients together for you in a package, which you, for example, would then take home and boil into a soup. You can smell the strong herbal fragrance whenever you walk into a Chinese drugstore.

Chinese medicines usually consider the body as a whole rather than focusing on specific ailments. A headache, for example, may be seen as evidence of an imbalance that is affecting your whole body, and the Chinese medicines will attempt to correct that general imbalance. This is related to the theory of *Yin* and *Yang* that we have discussed briefly in a previous lesson. Often, at a pharmacy the local staff can help suggest an appropriate Chinese medicine for you. Of course, for more serious illnesses you really should consult a doctor.

语言点

1. 浑身 whole body

打了两个小时的乒乓球，她浑身是汗。

She played ping-pong for two hours and was sweaty all over.

他没带雨伞，浑身都被淋湿了。

He didn't bring an umbrella and was wet from head to toe.

2. 偏要，不 intentionally against something, often with

让他别去那儿玩，他偏要去。

I don't allow him to play there, but he wants to go anyway.

你想知道这件事，我偏不告诉你。

You want to know about this. Well, I'm not going to tell you anyway.

句型 及 替换练习

别说……，连……也…… not just, even

别说外国人，连中国人也不认识这个字。

Not just foreigners, even Chinese don't recognize this character.

替换例句：

别说做饭了，他连开水也不会烧。

别说开汽车了，他连自行车也不会骑。

长城（1）

Great Wall（1）

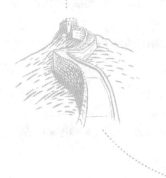

课文

小杰：爸爸，你知道 孟 姜 女的故事吗？
Xiǎo jié   Bà ba   nǐ zhī dào Mèng jiāng nǚ de gù shi ma

黄 人 豪：当 然 知 道 了。
Huáng Rén háo   Dāng rán zhī dào le

雪梅：人 豪，你 可 不 知 道，她 昨 天 上 课
Xuě méi   Rén háo   nǐ kě bù zhī dào   tā zuó tiān shàng kè

的 时 候 刚 学 了 这 个 故 事，今 天 逢
de shí hou gāng xué le zhè ge gù shi   jīn tiān féng

人 就 问。
rén jiù wèn

小 杰：爸 爸，你 既 然 知 道 这 个 故 事，就 带 我
Xiǎo jié   Bà ba   nǐ jì rán zhī dào zhè ge gù shi   jiù dài wǒ

去 长 城 玩 儿 吧，来 北 京 这 么 久，
qù Cháng chéng wánr ba   lái Běi jīng zhè me jiǔ

wǒ hái méi qù guo Cháng chéng ne
我还没去过长城呢。

Xuě méi　Lǎo gōng　wǒ zhèng zuó mo zhōu mò qù nǎr　ne
雪梅：老公，我正琢磨周末去哪儿呢？

Yào bù wǒ men jiù dài Xiǎo jié qù yí tàng Cháng chéng
要不我们就带小杰去一趟长城

ba
吧。

Xiǎo jié　Tài hǎo le　Bà ba　nǐ shuō wǒ men néng bù néng
小杰：太好了！爸爸，你说我们能不能

zhǎo dào dāng nián Mèng jiāng nǚ kū Cháng chéng de
找到当年孟姜女哭长城的

dì fang ne
地方呢？

Xuě méi　Nà zhǐ bú guò shì gè chuán shuō ér yǐ　nǐ hái dàng
雪梅：那只不过是个传说而已，你还当

zhēn le
真了。

Huáng Rén háo　Lái　Xiǎo jié　wǒ kǎo kao nǐ　nǐ zhī dào Mèng
黄人豪：来，小杰，我考考你，你知道孟

jiāng nǚ shì shén me cháo dài de rén ma
姜女是什么朝代的人吗？

Xiǎo jié　Ràng wǒ xiǎng xiang　nǐ nán bù dǎo wǒ de　shì
小杰：让我想想，你难不倒我的，是

Qín cháo de
秦朝的。

Huáng Rén háo　Duì a　ér wǒ men xiàn zài kě yǐ kān dào de Cháng
黄人豪：对啊，而我们现在可以看到的长

chéng zhǔ yào shì Míng dài xiū jiàn de
城主要是明代修建的。

Xiǎo jié　Zhè me shuō　chuán shuō lǐ de Cháng chéng hé xiàn
小杰：这么说，传说里的长城和现

zài kàn dào de Cháng chéng gēn běn jiù bú shì yì huí
在看到的长城根本就不是一回

shìr
事儿。

Huáng Rén háo　　Duì　nǐ zhēn cōng ming
黄 人 豪：对，你 真 聪 明。

Xuě méi　　Lǎo gōng　gāng cái nǐ shuō xiàn zài kàn dào de zhǔ
雪 梅：老 公， 刚 才 你 说 现 在 看 到 的 主

yào shì Míng Cháng chéng　nà me Míng cháo yǐ
要 是 明 长 城 ， 那 么 明 朝 以

hòu jiù bú zài xiū le ma
后 就 不 再 修 了 吗？

Huáng Rén háo　　Jī běn shì zhè yàng de　cóng Qīng cháo chū qī yǐ
黄 人 豪：基 本 是 这 样 的， 从 清 朝 初 期 以

hòu a　jiù bú zài xiū Cháng chéng le
后 啊， 就 不 再 修 长 城 了。

Xiǎo jié　　Nà wèi shén me ne
小 杰：那 为 什 么 呢？

Huáng Rén háo　　Xiǎng zhī dào dá àn a　nà wǒ xiān wèn nǐ yí gè
黄 人 豪：想 知 道 答 案 啊， 那 我 先 问 你 一 个

wèn tí　nǐ zhī dào wèi shén me yào xiū Cháng chéng
问 题，你 知 道 为 什 么 要 修 长 城

ma
吗？

Xiǎo jié　　Wǒ men lǎo shī shuō shì wèi le bāng zhù rén men dǎ
小 杰：我 们 老 师 说 是 为 了 帮 助 人 们 打

zhàng yòng de
仗 用 的。

Xuě méi　　Shuō shí huà　wǒ zhēn huái yí Cháng chéng zài zhàn
雪 梅：说 实 话，我 真 怀 疑 长 城 在 战

zhēng zhōng néng qǐ duō dà de zuò yòng
争 中 能 起 多 大 的 作 用。

Huáng Rén háo　　Zài yǐ qián　Cháng chéng dí què qǐ dào guo hěn
黄 人 豪：在 以 前， 长 城 的 确 起 到 过 很

dà de zuò yòng　kě shì dào le Qīng cháo　Cháng
大 的 作 用， 可 是 到 了 清 朝， 长

chéng jiù dǎng bú zhù xiàn dài de qiāng pào le
城 就 挡 不 住 现 代 的 枪 炮 了。

Xuě méi　　　O　　guài bu de Qīng cháo de shí hou yǐ jing bú zài
雪 梅：哦，怪 不 得 清 朝 的 时 候 已 经 不 再

xiū Cháng chéng le ne
修 长 城 了 呢。

Xiǎo jié　　Bà ba　　nǐ shuō Cháng chéng yǒu duō cháng a
小 杰：爸 爸，你 说 长 城 有 多 长 啊，

yǒu rén shuō zài Yuè qiú shang dōu néng kàn jiàn Cháng
有 人 说 在 月 球 上 都 能 看 见 长

chéng ne
城 呢。

Huáng Rén háo　　Xiǎng zhī dào Cháng chéng yǒu duō cháng　　nà nǐ qù
黄 人 豪：想 知 道 长 城 有 多 长，那 你 去

le yǐ hòu bú jiù zhī dào le ma
了 以 后 不 就 知 道 了 吗？

Xiǎo jié　　Tīng nǐ zhè me yì shuō　　wǒ dōu děng bù jí le
小 杰：听 你 这 么 一 说，我 都 等 不 及 了，

hèn bu de mǎ shàng jiù fēi guò qu kàn kan
恨 不 得 马 上 就 飞 过 去 看 看。

Huáng Rén háo　　Fēi　　Ha ha　　kàn nǐ　　dōu jí chéng zhè ge yàng
黄 人 豪：飞？哈 哈，看 你，都 急 成 这 个 样

zi le
子 了。

Xuě méi　　Chī wán fàn nǐ hái shi xiān qù xiě zuò yè ba　　Lí zhōu
雪 梅：吃 完 饭 你 还 是 先 去 写 作 业 吧。离 周

mò hái yǒu hǎo jǐ tiān ne
末 还 有 好 几 天 呢。

Xiǎo jié　　Hǎo ba　　xiàn zài kāi shǐ dǎo jì shí
小 杰：好 吧，现 在 开 始 倒 计 时。

Xiaojie: Dad, do you know the story of Mengjiangnu?

Huang Renhao: Of course I do.

Xuemei: You know what, since she learned the story in class yesterday, she keeps asking about it.

Xiaojie: Dad, can you take me to the Great Wall, since you know this story? I've been in Beijing for a while but I haven't been to the Great Wall.

Xuemei: Dear, I was wondering where to go at the weekend. Then, how about we take Xiaojie to the Great Wall?

Xiaojie: Great. Dad, do you think we can still find the place where Mengjiangnu's tears swept away the Great Wall?

Xuemei: That's only a legend. Don't take it seriously.

Huang Renhao: Come, Xiaojie. Let me test you. Do you know which dynasty Mengjiangnu was from?

Xiaojie: Let me see. You won't get me. Qin Dynasty (221BC−206BC).

Huang Renhao: Right. But the part of the Great Wall we see today was mainly built in the Ming Dynasty.

Xiaojie: Then, the Great Wall in the legend and the Great Wall we see today are totally different.

Huang Renhao: Yes. How clever you are!

Xuemei: Dear, just now you said that the part of the Great Wall we see today was mainly built in the Ming Dynasty. Does it mean that the wall-building completely stopped after that?

Huang Renhao: It's generally like that. Starting from the Qing Dynasty, no more of the Great Wall was built.

Xiaojie: Why?

Huang Renhao: Do you want to know the answer? Let me ask you a question first. Do you know why the Great Wall was built?

Xiaojie: Our teacher told us that it was used to help people in battle.

Xuemei: Frankly speaking, I really doubt the role the Great Wall played in war.

Huang Renhao: The Great Wall was very helpful before the Qing Dynasty. But after that, with the coming of guns and cannons, it became useless by the Qing Dynasty.

Xuemei: Oh, no wonder the wall-building stopped in the Qing Dynasty.

Xiaojie: Dad, how long is the Great Wall? It is said you can even see it from the moon.

Huang Renhao: If you really want to know, go and see it for yourself.

Xiaojie: After what you've said, I can't wait. I have an urge to fly there right away.

Huang Renhao: Fly? Haha, look, how excited you are!

Xuemei: After dinner, go and do your homework. There are several days to go before the weekend.

Xiaojie: OK, let's count down now.

生词

1.	故事	gù shi	名	story
2.	长城	Cháng chéng	名	the Great Wall
3.	传说	chuán shuō	名	legend
4.	考	kǎo	动	test
5.	朝代	cháo dài	名	dynasty
6.	秦朝	Qín cháo	名	the Qin Dynasty
7.	修建	xiū jiàn	动	build
8.	明朝	Míng cháo	名	the Ming Dynasty
9.	初期	chū qī	名	early period
10.	答案	dá àn	名	answer
11.	打仗	dǎ zhàng	动	fight
12.	怀疑	huái yí	动	doubt
13.	战争	zhàn zhēng	名	war
14.	作用	zuò yòng	名	effect
15.	挡	dǎng	动	resist
16.	枪炮	qiāng pào	名	firearm
17.	月球	Yuè qiú	名	moon
18.	作业	zuò yè	名	homework
19.	倒计时	dào jì shí	动	count down

注释

1. 逢人就问。

○ 逢 is to encounter, to come across. 逢人就问 is to ask whoever you come across. 他逢人就说, he says this to whoever he meets.

2. 你既然知道这个故事，就带我去长城玩儿吧。

○ Given that you know this tale, then why don't you take me to the Great Wall for some fun. Here Xiaojie uses the sentence pattern "既然 sth. 就 sth. else", which is like "since or given that sth., then sth. else".

3. 我正琢磨周末去哪儿呢？要不我们就带小杰去一趟长城吧。

○ 琢磨 means to think about, or to ponder. 咱们就去长城吧, let's go to the Great Wall. Notice how she uses 吧 to indicate a suggestion.

4. 那只不过是个传说而已。

○ That is nothing but a fable. This is similar to saying 那只是个传说, that is only a fable. But this sentence structure "只不过 sth. 而已" is much more emphatic. It's used to minimize or sometimes even to belittle something, to make something smaller.

5. 你难不倒我的。

○ 倒 is to topple or to overturn. For example, 摔倒, to fall over. Here it's used at a very abstract sense. 难不倒 means to not be able to stump somebody. 你难不倒我的, you can't stump me.

6. 我都等不及了，恨不得马上就飞过去看看。

○ I can't wait any longer. I wish I could fly over now and take a look. 恨不得 expresses a very strong desire or a wish.

文化
背景

The Tale of Mengjiangnu

The story dates from the Qin Dynasty, when China was first unified into one country over 2000 years ago. This is the time when smaller walls from various kingdoms were joined into one Great Wall under the orders of Qin Shihuang, the first emperor of China. He is regarded in Chinese history as a great military leader who unified China, but also a very cruel and harsh leader. At this time, many people were conscripted into the army against their will and treated as slave labour.

Mengjiangnu was a beautiful woman who lived in Jiangsu Province, far from the capital of China at the time and also far from the Great Wall, which ran along the northern boundary of the empire. She had just been married a few days when her husband was suddenly conscripted into the army and taken away by force. Their young marriage was torn apart, and Meng Jiangnu cried every day.

Months later, as winter arrived, she prepared some winter clothing for her husband and started off to find him. It was a long journey to the northern regions so far from her home, and at first she had no idea where she might find him. Eventually, she met some labourers who told her that they had worked with her husband building the Great Wall nearby. When she asked of his whereabouts, she was told that he had died just a month ago from exhaustion and starvation. So many workers had died during the building of the wall that they were forced to simply bury the bodies inside the wall as it was built.

Mengjiangnu went to this place along the wall and cried and cried for several days. This is what we call 哭长城, she cried before the wall. Suddenly there was a loud crack and the wall broke open. She found the remains of her husband along with all the other workers, and was thus able at least to give him a proper burial. It's a story of undying love, and the power of love to overcome all obstacles.

语言点

1. 的确，确实 really, indeed

四川菜的确很辣。

Sichuan food is quite hot.

2. 根本 simply, fundamentally

今年冬天根本就不冷。

It's not cold at all this winter.

句型 及 替换练习

1. V+不及 action can't be achieved

北京烤鸭有你说得那么好吃吗？我已经等不及要去尝尝了。

Is Peking Duck really as good as you say? I can hardly wait to taste it.

替换例句：

今天起晚了，我来不及吃早饭了。

他都等不及我把这句话说完就跑出去了。

2. ……而已 nothing more

我只不过随便说说而已，你还当真了。

I was just speaking casually. You took it seriously.

别生气，只是开个玩笑而已！

Don't be angry. We were just kidding.

替换例句：

我只是随便看看而已，并不真想买什么东西。

我只是提个建议而已，该怎么办还得你自己拿主意。

第 *10* 课

长城 (2)

Great Wall (2)

课文

Xiǎo jié　Bà ba　　kuài diǎnr
小 杰：爸爸，快 点儿。

Huáng Rén háo　Xiǎo jié　xiǎo xīn　nǐ màn diǎnr　a
黄 人 豪：小 杰，小 心，你 慢 点儿 啊。

Xiǎo jié　Bà ba　nǐ kàn　zhè Cháng chéng dōu xiū zài shān
小 杰：爸爸，你 看，这 长 城 都 修 在 山
shang　yuè lái yuè gāo
上 ，越 来 越 高。

Huáng Rén háo　Piào liang ba　gāo dī qǐ fú de　jiù xiàng yì tiáo
黄 人 豪：漂 亮 吧，高 低 起伏 的，就 像 一 条
lóng shì de
龙 似 的。

Xiǎo jié　Piào liang　bǐ wǒ zài zhào piàn lǐ kàn dào de hái
小 杰：漂 亮，比 我 在 照 片 里 看 到 的 还
hǎo kàn
好 看。

Huáng Rén háo　Shì a　Xiǎo jié a　zán men jì xù wǎng shàng pá
黄 人 豪：是 啊，小 杰 啊，咱 们 继续 往 上 爬

bā shàng bian de fēng jǐng gèng měi lì zǒu
吧，上 边 的 风 景 更 美 丽。走！

Xiǎo jié Bà ba Cháng chéng shàng bian yě hǎo kuān na
小 杰：爸爸，长 城 上 边 也 好 宽 呐！

Wǒ men kě yǐ zài zhèr jǔ bàn gè
我 们 可 以 在 这 儿 举 办 个 party。

Huáng Rén háo Nà kě bù xíng Xiǎo jié Cháng chéng shì guó jiā
黄 人 豪：那 可 不 行。小 杰，长 城 是 国 家

zhòng diǎn bǎo hù wén wù Nǐ zhī dào ma Zhè li kě
重 点 保 护 文 物。你 知 道 吗 ？这 里 可

yǐ tóng shí zǒu wǔ pǐ mǎ shí gè shì bīng ne
以 同 时 走 五 匹 马、十 个 士 兵 呢。

Xiǎo jié Bà ba nǐ kuài lái kàn zhè Cháng chéng de zhuān
小 杰：爸爸，你 快 来 看，这 长 城 的 砖

kě zhēn gòu dà de Nǐ shuō zhè xiē zhuān shì zěn me
可 真 够 大 的。你 说 这 些 砖 是 怎 么

bān shàng lái de Ér qiě yòu méi yǒu qì chē bān
搬 上 来 的 ？而 且 又 没 有 汽 车，搬

zhè xiē zhuān děi duō fèi jìn ya
这 些 砖 得 多 费 劲 呀。

Huáng Rén háo Bié shuō qì chē le zhè li lián tiáo lù dōu méi yǒu
黄 人 豪：别 说 汽 车 了，这 里 连 条 路 都 没 有。

Yào zhī dào zhè li de shān zuì gāo yǒu duō mǐ
要 知 道 这 里 的 山 最 高 有 1000 多 米

ne quán shì kào rén yí kuài yí kuài bān shàng lái de
呢，全 是 靠 人 一 块 一 块 搬 上 来 的。

Xiǎo jié Wa zhēn liǎo bu qǐ Ai bà ba nǐ shuō yǒu
小 杰：哇，真 了 不 起。哎，爸爸，你 说 有

rén zǒu dào guò Cháng chéng de tóur ma
人 走 到 过 长 城 的 头 儿 吗 ？

Huáng Rén háo Yǒu a yǒu rén cóng Shān hǎi guān yì zhí zǒu dào Jiā
黄 人 豪：有 啊，有 人 从 山 海 关 一 直 走 到 嘉

yù guān
峪 关。

Xiǎo jié　Nà děi zǒu duō cháng shí jiān ne
小 杰：那 得 走 多 长 时 间 呢？

Huáng Rén háo　Zhì shǎo děi zǒu liǎng gè yuè
黄 人 豪：至 少 得 走 两 个 月。

Xiǎo jié　A　zhè me cháng a　yào shi wǒ cái zǒu bú dòng ne
小 杰：啊，这 么 长 啊，要 是 我 才 走 不 动 呢。

Bà ba　nǐ gāng cái shuō de nǎ liǎng gè guān jiù shì
爸 爸，你 刚 才 说 的 那 两 个 关 就 是

Cháng chéng de liǎng tóur　ba
长 城 的 两 头 儿 吧？

Huáng Rén háo　Duì a　nǐ shì zěn me cāi dào de
黄 人 豪：对 啊，你 是 怎 么 猜 到 的？

Xiǎo jié　Shén me cāi de　shì wǒ shàng wǎng chá de　Wǎng
小 杰：什 么 猜 的，是 我 上 网 查 的。 网

shàng hái shuō Cháng chéng de yì tóu zài hǎi li ne
上 还 说 长 城 的 一 头 在 海 里 呢。

Huáng Rén háo　You　zhè me rèn zhēn a
黄 人 豪：呦，这 么 认 真 啊。

Xiǎo jié　Nà dāng rán le　Lǎo shī hái ràng wǒ men xiě yì piān
小 杰：那 当 然 了。老 师 还 让 我 们 写 一 篇

guān yú Cháng chéng de zuò wén ne
关 于 长 城 的 作 文 呢。

Huáng Rén háo　Xiǎo jié　nǐ kàn nà me gāo de dì fang hái yǒu rén
黄 人 豪：小 杰，你 看 那 么 高 的 地 方 还 有 人，

zán men yě pá shàng qu kàn kan ba
咱 们 也 爬 上 去 看 看 吧！

Xiǎo jié　Nà me gāo a
小 杰：那 么 高 啊？

Huáng Rén háo　Xiǎo jié　nǐ kàn zán men lái bǐ sài　kàn shuí xiān
黄 人 豪：小 杰，你 看 咱 们 来 比 赛，看 谁 先

dào shān dǐng　hǎo bù hǎo
到 山 顶，好 不 好？

Xiǎo jié　Bǐ sài　Nà wǒ yíng dìng le
小 杰：比 赛？那 我 赢 定 了！

Xiaojie: Come on dad, hurry up!

Huang Renhao: Xiaojie, be careful, slow down a bit.

Xiaojie: Dad, look how the Great Wall is built on the mountain and goes higher and higher.

Huang Renhao: Isn't it beautiful—rising and falling, like a dragon?

Xiaojie: It is beautiful, even better than the Great Wall I've seen in photographs.

Huang Renhao: Come on, let's keep climbing up. The view's even more beautiful up there. Let't go!

Xiaojie: Dad, the top of the Great Wall is really wide, we could have a party up here.

Huang Renhao: I don't think so. Xiaojie, the Great Wall is a protected National Heritage site. Up here five horses and ten soldiers could stand side by side.

Xiaojie: Dad, come and have a look at the huge bricks of the Great Wall. How do you think they moved these bricks up here? They didn 't have any trucks, so it would have been so hard to move the bricks here.

Huang Renhao: There weren't even roads up here on the mountain, not

to mention trucks. The highest mountain here is over 1000 metres. All the bricks were carried up by man—one by one.

Xiaojie: That's really something! Hey, do you think anyone's ever walked to the end of the Great Wall?

Huang Renhao: Sure, some people have walked from Shanhai Guan all the way to Jiayu Guan.

Xiaojie: How long would that take?

Huang Renhao: You'd walk for at least two months.

Xiaojie: Oh, that long, I wouldn't be able to walk that far. Dad, the two passes or "guan" you just mentioned are the two ends of the Great Wall, right?

Huang Renhao: That's right, how did you guess?

Xiaojie: Guess? I looked it up on the Internet. It also says on the Internet that one end of the Great Wall is in the sea.

Huang Renhao: Well, aren't you serious?

Xiaojie: Of course. Our teacher wants us to write an essay on the Great Wall.

Huang Renhao: Xiaojie, look, there are even people up there, let's climb up and have a look.

Xiaojie: So high?

Huang Renhao: Xiaojie, let's have a race to see who can get to the top first!

Xiaojie: I'll win for sure!

生词

1.	起伏	qǐ fú	动	rise and fall
2.	像……似的	xiàng…shì de		similar to
3.	继续	jì xù	动	continue
4.	美丽	měi lì	形	beautiful
5.	宽	kuān	形	wide
6.	举办	jǔ bàn	动	hold
7.	国家	guó jiā	名	country
8.	重点	zhòng diǎn	名	focal point, key
9.	保护	bǎo hù	动	protect
10.	文物	wén wù	名	cultural relics
11.	砖	zhuān	名	brick
12.	搬	bān	动	move
13.	费劲	fèi jìn	动	make great efforts
14.	靠	kào	动	depend on
15.	了不起	liǎo bu qǐ	形	great
16.	头儿	tóur	名	end
17.	至少	zhì shǎo	副	at least
18.	上网	shàng wǎng	动	surf the Internet
19.	海	hǎi	名	sea
20.	认真	rèn zhēn	形	serious, conscientious
21.	作文	zuò wén	名	essay
22.	比赛	bǐ sài	名	race
23.	山顶	shān dǐng	名	mountain peak

注释

1. 高低起伏的，就像一条龙似的。

○ 高低 is high and low. 起伏 means to rise and fall. 像一条龙似的, it looks like a dragon, another traditional symbol of China.

2. 咱们继续往上爬吧。

○ Let's keep on climbing up. Remember how I said we usually use the term 爬长城, climb the Great Wall.

3. 这里可以同时走五匹马、十个士兵呢。

○ It is said that 5 horses or 10 soldiers can walk across, side by side. This was useful for moving large armies into position to fend off an invasion.

4. 别说汽车了，这里连条路都没有。

○ 条 is the measure word for roads as well as other things that are long and thin. In English, we usually reverse the order to say "there weren't even roads on the mountain, much less automobiles". 别说 sth., 连 sth. else, don't even mention that, even something else.

5. （古代的中国人）真了不起。

○ (Ancient Chinese) were really quite amazing. 了不起 is a colloquial expression, similar to 真棒, that's great.

6. 有人从山海关一直走到嘉峪关。

○ 山海关 and 嘉峪关 are two of the most famous gates in the wall, one in the far east on the shore of the Bohai Sea and one in the western regions of China. 山海关, literally mountain and sea gate, is where the Great Wall meets the Bohai Sea.

7. 至少得走两个月。

○ You would have to walk at least two months. 至少 means the minimum amount. It's the opposite of 最多.

8. 那我赢定了！

○ I will surely win. 定了 means it has already been determined.

Great Wall

In Chinese we call it 万里长城, 10000 li wall, but actually the Great Wall extends about 6000 kilometers. It was first built over 2000 years ago, then repaired and rebuilt several times at different stages in Chinese history, up to the Ming Dynasty, around 600 years ago. So the wall is not one complete line, but a series of walls that follow the same general path. Some areas are easily visible, and have been restored to their former glory, and others are almost completely buried or destroyed.

Of course, the Great Wall was initially built to keep invaders out of China on China's northern boundary. There are high towers where fires would be lit to send signals warning of invasion. These are called 烽火台. Horses and men could then be moved very quickly along the wall to counter any attack. Passes were also built through this artificial barrier. For instance, 居庸关 the Juyong Pass near Beijing, is among them. You'll pass through this or you'll drive by it on your way to Badaling, which is probably the most common site to visit on the wall. These parts of the wall date back to the Ming Dynasty and have been restored to their original condition. While they are now maintained as a tourist destination, the authorities are eager to preserve the wall. For example, there is a pass through the wall which is only wide enough for one car or one lane, yet strict regulations will not allow this pass to be widened. Now there are still many parts of the wall that you can see today in their unrestored state, for instance at a place called Jiankou, one of the most scenic stretches of the Great Wall near Beijing. It is also known as one of the most photographed stretches of the wall. However, getting there is a little bit difficult. It's almost impossible if you don't have a car or you aren't an experienced driver. Because most of the wall here is in ruins, the climb itself is extremely dangerous. After all, the wall follows a path right over the mountains, not around them. But if you want to see the real thing, this is as real as it gets!

旅游汉语

语言点

1. 至少 at least

从这儿打车去机场，至少要80块钱。

To take a taxi from here to the airport, it needs at least 80 RMB.

他看上去至少有50多岁了。

It seems that he's at least 50 years old.

2. 刚才 just now, just then

你刚才说什么来着，我没听清楚。

What did you say just now? I didn't hear clearly.

这件事儿你为什么刚才不说，而现在才说？

Why didn't you mention this thing before? Why are you only saying it now?

3. 了不起 extraordinary, amazing

他那么小就会说两门外语，了不起！

He's so small, yet he already speaks two foreign languages. It's really amazing.

2000年前就能修长城，这是一件很了不起的事情！

To build the Great Wall 2000 years ago is an amazing achievement.

句型 及 替换练习

像……一样/似的 just like, similar to

她笑起来很可爱，像个天使似的。

She looks really cute when she smiles, just like an angel.

替换例句：

长城看起来像一条龙。

她走路的样子就像在跳舞似的。

第11课

颐和园（1）
Summer Palace (1)

课文

Xiǎo Wáng	Ā yí Liú Yǒng zài ma
小 王 ：阿姨，刘 勇 在 吗？

Biǎo jiě	Tā chū qù mǎi běn shū yí huìr jiù huí lái nǐ
表 姐：他 出 去 买 本 书，一 会儿 就 回来，你

xiān jìn lái děng tā yí huìr ba
先 进 来 等 他 一 会儿 吧。

Xiǎo Wáng	Hǎo de xiè xie ā yí
小 王 ：好 的，谢谢 阿姨。

Biǎo jiě	Lái wǒ lái gěi nǐ men jiè shào yí xià zhè shì Liú
表 姐：来，我 来 给 你 们 介绍 一 下，这 是 刘

Yǒng de biǎo mèi Xiǎo jié Xiǎo jié zhè shì Liú
勇 的 表 妹，小 杰。 小 杰，这 是 刘

Yǒng de tóng xué Xiǎo Wáng gē ge
勇 的 同 学，小 王 哥哥。

Xiǎo jié　Gē ge hǎo
小 杰：哥哥好！

Xiǎo Wáng　Nǐ hǎo
小 王：你好！

Biǎo jié　Qǐng zuò　Xiǎo Wáng a　wǒ jué de nǐ píng shí tǐng
表 姐：请 坐！小 王 啊，我 觉 得 你 平 时 挺

jīng shen de　zěn me jīn tiān kàn qǐ lái zhè me wú jīng
精 神 的，怎 么 今 天 看 起 来 这 么 无 精

dǎ cǎi de
打 采 的？

Xiǎo Wáng　Bié tí le　zuó tiān liǎng diǎn duō cái shuì
小 王：别 提 了，昨 天 两 点 多 才 睡。

Biǎo jié　You　kāi yè chē a　zhè duì shēn tǐ kě bù hǎo
表 姐：呦，开 夜 车 啊，这 对 身 体 可 不 好。

Xiǎo jié　Shì a　ér qiě wǎn shang kāi chē　yě hěn wēi xiǎn
小 杰：是 啊，而 且 晚 上 开 车，也 很 危 险。

Biǎo jié　Ha ha　Xiǎo jié　zhè　kāi yè chē　jiù shì wǎn
表 姐：哈 哈，小 杰，这"开 夜 车"就 是 晚

shang bú shuì jiào de yì si　gēn yè li kāi chē
上 不 睡 觉 的 意 思，跟 夜 里 开 车

méi guān xi
没 关 系。

Xiǎo jié　Shì zhè me huí shìr　a　yǒu yì si　Nà nǐ wèi
小 杰：是 这 么 回 事 儿 啊，有 意 思。那 你 为

shén me yào kāi yè chē ne
什 么 要 开 夜 车 呢？

Xiǎo Wáng　Wǒ men lǎo shī gěi wǒ chū le dào nán tí　fēi yào ràng
小 王：我 们 老 师 给 我 出 了 道 难 题，非 要 让

wǒ jīn tiān péi wài jiào qù Yí hé Yuán　suǒ yǐ wǒ yì
我 今 天 陪 外 教 去 颐 和 园，所 以 我 一

zhí zài chá zī liào　è bǔ zhè fāng miàn de zhī shi
直 在 查 资 料，恶 补 这 方 面 的 知 识。

Biǎo jié　Nà jīn tiān wài jiào hái mǎn yì ma
表 姐：那 今 天 外 教 还 满 意 吗？

小 王：Xiǎo Wáng
Nà hái yòng shuō wǒ men wài jiào shuō dào mù qián
那还用说，我们外教说，到目前
wèi zhǐ wǒ shì tā yù dào de zuì hǎo de dǎo yóu ne
为止，我是他遇到的最好的导游呢。

表 姐：Biǎo jiě
Nǐ hái zhēn yǒu liǎng xià zi
你还真有两下子！

小 王：Xiǎo Wáng
Bú shì kāi wán xiào wǒ xiàn zài dōu kě yǐ dāng Yí hé
不是开玩笑，我现在都可以当颐和
Yuán de dǎo yóu le
园的导游了。

小 杰：Xiǎo jié
Hǎo a zhōu mò wǒ hé mā ma yào yì qǐ qù Yí hé
好啊，周末我和妈妈要一起去颐和
Yuán nǐ néng dāng wǒ men de dǎo yóu ma
园，你能当我们的导游吗？

表 姐：Biǎo jiě
Ai duì le zhèng hǎo Liú Yǒng zhōu mò yào qù xué
哎，对了，正好刘勇周末要去学
chē bù néng hé tā men yí kuàir qù nǐ yào shi
车，不能和她们一块儿去，你要是
néng péi tā men qù nà kě jiù tài hǎo le
能陪她们去那可就太好了。

小 王：Xiǎo Wáng
Méi wèn tí xiǎo shì yì zhuāng bāo zài wǒ shēn
没问题，小事一桩，包在我身
shang bǎo zhèng ràng nǐ men mǎn yì
上，保证让你们满意。

小 杰：Xiǎo jié
Gē ge Yí hé Yuán shì bú shì tǐng dà de
哥哥，颐和园是不是挺大的？

小 王：Xiǎo Wáng
Shì a bú guò dà jiā qù Yí hé Yuán bú shì yīn wèi
是啊，不过大家去颐和园不是因为
tā dà zhǔ yào shì yīn wèi tā kě yǐ kàn de dōng xi
它大，主要是因为它可以看的东西
tài duō le
太多了。

小杰：Nà qù Yí hé Yuán zhǔ yào yīng gāi kàn shén me ne
那去颐和园主要应该看什么呢？

小王：Gēn jù wǒ de diào chá Yí hé Yuán shì Zhōng guó
根据我的调查，颐和园是中国
yuán lín yì shù de dài biǎo Rú guǒ nǐ xiǎng liǎo jiě
园林艺术的代表。如果你想了解
Zhōng guó yuán lín wén huà kàn kan Yí hé Yuán jiù
中国园林文化，看看颐和园就
gòu le
够了。

小杰：Yǒu nà me hǎo ma Tīng qǐ lái xiàng guǎng gào yí yàng
有那么好吗？听起来像广告一样。

小王：Wǒ kě méi chuī niú nǐ men qīn zì qù kàn kan jiù zhī
我可没吹牛，你们亲自去看看就知
dào le
道了。

小杰：Yì yán wéi dìng wǒ Xīng qī liù lái zhǎo nǐ
一言为定，我星期六来找你。

小王：Méi wèn tí
没问题！

Xiao Wang: Aunt, is Liu Yong around?

Cousin: He's gone out to buy a book. He'll be back in a little while. Why don't you come in and wait for him?

Xiao Wang: OK, thanks aunt.

Cousin: Here, let me introduce you to Xiaojie, Liu Yong's cousin. Xiaojie, this is Xiao Wang, Liu Yong's school friend.

Xiaojie: Hello, Xiao wang!

Xiao Wang: Hello!

Cousin: Have a seat please Xiao Wang, you're usually pretty full of life. Why do you look so worn out today?

Xiao Wang: Don't ask, I didn't get to bed until two a.m. yesterday.

Cousin: Oh, night-driving. That's not good for your health.

Xiaojie: Yes. Besides, night-driving is very dangerous.

Cousin: Haha, Xiaojie, "night driving" means not sleeping at night. It has nothing to do with driving.

Xiaojie: Oh right, interesting. Then why did you do that?

Xiao Wang: Our teacher gave me a tough task. I had to take our international teacher to the Summer Palace today, so I was studying up on the subject.

Cousin: Well, was the international teacher pleased?

Xiao Wang: Naturally. Our international teacher said I was the best tour guide he's ever met.

Cousin: You're really good!

Xiao Wang: No kidding, I really can be a Summer Palace tour guide now.

Xiaojie: That's perfect. My mother and I are going to the Summer Palace this weekend. Can you be our tour guide?

Cousin: Oh right. It happens Liu Yong has driving lessons this weekend and can't go with them. If you could go with them instead that would be great.

Xiao Wang: No problem, a piece of cake. I'll take care of it, satisfaction guaranteed.

Xiaojie: Xiao Wang, is the Summer Palace really huge?

Xiao Wang: Yes. But people go there not mainly because of its size. It's because there's so much to see there.

Xiaojie: Then what do you mainly see at the Summer Palace?

Xiao Wang: According to my research, the Summer Palace is a prime example of Chinese landscape design. If you want to know about China's landscape culture, just take a look at the Summer Palace.

Xiaojie: Is it really so great? Sounds like an advertisement.

Xiao Wang: I'm not bragging, you can see for yourself.

Xiaojie: It's a deal then. I'll come and meet you on Saturday.

Xiao Wang: Sure!

生词

1.	阿姨	ā yí	名	aunt
2.	哥哥	gē ge	名	elder brother
3.	精神	jīng shen	形	vigorous
4.	无精打采	wú jīng dǎ cǎi	形	in low spirits
5.	开夜车	kāi yè chē		burn the midnight oil
6.	危险	wēi xiǎn	形	dangerous
7.	难题	nán tí	名	difficult problem
8.	外教	wài jiào	名	international teacher
9.	资料	zī liào	名	material
10.	恶补	è bǔ	动	cram
11.	知识	zhī shi	名	knowledge
12.	满意	mǎn yì	形	satisfied
13.	导游	dǎo yóu	名	tour guide
14.	小事一桩	xiǎo shì yì zhuāng		a piece of cake
15.	园林	yuán lín	名	garden
16.	代表	dài biǎo	名	representative
17.	了解	liǎo jiě	动	know

注释

1. 怎么今天看起来这么无精打采的？
   ⟳ Here, the 精 character is the same as in 精神, but it's preceded by 无, which means 没有, to not have.

2. 老师给我出了道难题。
   ⟳ 道 is the measure word for 问题, a question, or 难题, which should be a difficult problem.

3. 恶补
   ⟳ 恶补 is to cram something in a very short period of time.

4. 到目前为止，我是他遇到的最好的导游呢。
   ⟳ 到目前为止, up to now, up to the present. 止 literally means to stop, so stopping now , up to the present.

5. 你还真有两下子！
   ⟳ This is a colloquial expression like "to have a trick or two up your sleeve".

6. 小事一桩，包在我身上。
   ⟳ 桩 is a measure word for piece, a piece of cake, a small task. We can also use the measure word 件, 小事一件. That's the same meaning. 包在我身上, I'll take it upon myself. I'll do it myself.

7. 园林
   ⟳ 园林 is a garden or park area, 园林艺术 can mean the art of landscaping or gardening.

8. 我可没吹牛。
   ⟳ It's not just boasting. Here, 吹 is short for 吹牛, to boast.

9. 一言为定
   ⟳ Then it's settled, it's agreed. 一言为定 indicates a verbal agreement. 一言为定, one word sets the agreement.

Summer Palace

The Summer Palace, 颐和园, is one of the best sites in the Beijing area. In the later part of the last dynasty, the imperial family would often come here during the summer months to avoid the heat of the Forbidden City. Relief from the heat is mainly due to Kunming Lake, which occupies about three fourths of the park. Much of this lake is man-made, with the soil excavated being used to increase the size of 万寿山, Longevity Hill, on the north side of the lake.

The park is firmly linked in history with the Empress Dowager Cixi, who was the true source of power in the late Qing Dynasty. She is seen as a corrupt figure who prevented China from taking the necessary steps to modernize. For example, it is said that she built a marble boat on the shores of Kunming Lake. Of course, the boat doesn't float. It's simply a place where you can lounge about and enjoy the scenery. Several years later after this boat was built, China again found herself unable to defend against foreign aggression.

There is a central building in the Summer Palace where the emperor would deal with state business while residing at the Summer Palace. It is said, however, that the Empress Dowager would sit behind a screen right behind the emperor, so that she could tell him what to do. This is called 垂帘听政, to sit behind the screen and order the business of the day.

Besides the lake and the marble boat, one of the most interesting sites at the Summer Palace is the 700 metres long covered walkway called 长廊 that is mentioned in the dialogue. There is also a beautiful stone bridge called 十七孔桥, 17-span bridge that links the main island to the shore. Near the bridge you will find a beautiful bronze ox who seems to be leisurely enjoying the scenery. If you are in Beijing for more than just a day or two, this is definitely a site worth seeing.

语言点

1. 主要 main, primary

上海是中国的主要城市之一。

Shanghai is one of the main cities in China.

水果的价格主要是由季节来决定的。

The price of fruits is mainly determined by the season.

2. 根据 according to

根据气象部门预测，未来两天将有大风。

According to the prediction of the weather department, it would be windy over the next two days.

句型 及 替换练习

1. 到……为止 up to a certain point

到目前为止，我至少已经去过20多个国家了。

Up to this point, I've been to at least 20 countries.

替换例句：

到现在为止，我还没找到解决问题的办法。

到今天为止，我已经在中国待了整整一年了。

2. 有两下子 to know a trick or two

他修车很有两下子。

He's very skillful at fixing cars.

替换例句：

没有两下子，是不可能当上老板的。

他办事儿真有两下子。

第 *12* 课

颐和园 (2)

Summer Palace (2)

旅游汉语

课文

Xuě méi　　Xiǎo Wáng a　　　zǎo jiù xiǎng dào Yí hé Yuán lái
雪梅： 小 王 啊，早 就 想 到 颐 和 园 来

wánr　　xiè xie nǐ jīn tiān péi wǒ men yì qǐ lái
玩儿，谢 谢 你 今 天 陪 我 们 一 起 来。

Xiǎo Wáng　　Nǐ bié zhè me shuō　　nǐ tài kè qi le
小 王： 你 别 这 么 说，你 太 客 气 了。

Xiǎo jié　　Gē ge　　zhè me duō mén　　wǒ men yīng gāi cóng nǎ
小 杰： 哥 哥，这 么 多 门，我 们 应 该 从 哪

yí gè jìn qù ne
一 个 进 去 呢？

Xiǎo Wáng　　Zhè ge jiào Dōng gōng mén　　shì Yí hé Yuán de zhèng
小 王： 这 个 叫 东 宫 门，是 颐 和 园 的 正

mén　　Mén kǒu de zhèng zhōng jiān dāng nián kě shì
门。门 口 的 正 中 间 当 年 可 是

huáng dì hé Cí xǐ tài hòu cái kě yǐ zǒu de　　 qí tā
皇帝和慈禧太后才可以走的，其他

de rén yào xiǎng cóng zhèr zǒu　　 nà kě méi ménr
的人要想从这儿走，那可没门儿。

Xiǎo jié　　Nà tā men dōu zǒu nǎr　 a
小杰：那他们都走哪儿啊？

Xiǎo Wáng　　Tā men zhǐ néng zǒu liǎng biān de xiǎo ménr
小王：他们只能走两边的小门儿。

Xuě méi　　Méi xiǎng dào zhè mén hái huì yǒu zhè me duō de jiǎng
雪梅：没想到这门还会有这么多的讲

jiū　　Zán men zǒu ba
究。咱们走吧。

Xiǎo jié　　Wa　　zhè li kě zhēn dà a　　 gē ge　　 wǒ men gāi
小杰：哇，这里可真大啊，哥哥，我们该

cháo nǎ ge fāng xiàng cái hǎo
朝哪个方向才好？

Xiǎo Wáng　　Wǎng zhè biān　　gēn wǒ zǒu　　Xiǎo jié　　 nǐ bié kàn
小王：往这边，跟我走。小杰，你别看

Yí hé yuán zhè me dà　　 qí shí tā shì yóu sān gè bù
颐和园这么大，其实它是由三个部

fen zǔ chéng de
分组成的。

Xiǎo jié　　Nǎ sān gè bù fen ne
小杰：哪三个部分呢？

Xiǎo Wáng　　Gōng tíng qū　　Wàn shòu shān hé Kūn míng hú　　Nǐ
小王：宫廷区、万寿山和昆明湖。你

men xiǎng kàn nǎ gè bù fen ne
们想看哪个部分呢？

Xuě méi　　Zhè xiē wǒ men dōu xiǎng kàn　　dàn bù zhī xiān kàn nǎ
雪梅：这些我们都想看，但不知先看哪

ge hǎo
个好？

小杰：我想看宫廷区。那是不是皇帝住的地方？

小王：宫廷区当年是皇帝和慈禧太后办公的地方，在那儿你还可以看到慈禧太后的寝宫。

小杰：寝宫？那是什么地方？

小王："寝"就是睡觉的意思，寝宫就是皇帝和太后休息的地方。

雪梅：慈禧和皇帝住在颐和园？他们不是住在故宫里吗？

小杰：他们不是偶尔来这里度假的吧？

小王：不是这样的，慈禧太后就很喜欢住在这里，有时候她一住就是大半年呢。

小杰：哦，原来是这样啊。

雪梅：这就是著名的长廊了吧？我以

qián jīng cháng zài míng xìn piàn shàng kàn dào tā
前 经 常 在 明 信 片 上 看 到 它。

Xiǎo jié
小 杰：Zhè xiē huà de dōu shì shén me a Wǒ dōu kàn bù
这 些 画 的 都 是 什 么 啊？我 都 看 不
dǒng
懂！

Xiǎo Wáng
小 王：Zhè lǐ bian yǒu de wǒ dōu kàn bù dǒng Zhè lǐ bian
这 里 边 有 的 我 都 看 不 懂 。 这 里 边
yǒu de huà de shì Xī hú fēng jǐng yǒu de shì mín jiān
有 的 画 的 是 西 湖 风 景 ， 有 的 是 民 间
gù shi
故 事 。

Xuě méi
雪 梅：Wǒ jué de zhè Cháng láng shè jì de hěn bú cuò bù
我 觉 得 这 长 廊 设 计 得 很 不 错， 不
jǐn fēn gé le zhè biān de shān hé hú ér qiě
仅 分 隔 了 这 边 的 山 和 湖 ， 而 且
kàn fēng jǐng de shí hou hái kě yǐ fáng yǔ fáng shài
看 风 景 的 时 候 还 可 以 防 雨 防 晒 。

Xiǎo Wáng
小 王：Nǐ hái zhēn shuō dào diǎn zi shàng le dí què shì zhè
你 还 真 说 到 点 子 上 了，的 确 是 这
yàng de
样 的 。

Xiǎo jié
小 杰：Mā ma nǐ kàn nà biān de hú zhēn piào liang
妈 妈， 你 看， 那 边 的 湖 真 漂 亮！

Xiǎo Wáng
小 王：Zhè jiù shì Kūn míng hú Tā de xíng zhuàng kàn qǐ lái
这 就 是 昆 明 湖。它 的 形 状 看 起 来
xiàng gè shòu táo ér hòu mian de Wàn shòu shān ne
像 个 寿 桃，而 后 面 的 万 寿 山 呢，
tā de xíng zhuàng xiàng yì zhī biān fú
它 的 形 状 像 一 只 蝙 蝠 。

Xiǎo jié
小 杰：Biān fú Wèi shén me piān piān yào xiàng biān fú
蝙 蝠？ 为 什 么 偏 偏 要 像 蝙 蝠
ne Duō nán kàn a
呢？ 多 难 看 啊？

小王：不知道了吧，这是因为蝙蝠的

"蝠"和幸福的"福"发音是一样的。

雪梅：这样设计都是为了图个吉利吧？

小王：固然有这方面的考虑，不过这也

反映出中国园林的一大特点。

小杰：听不懂，听不懂，我们现在去爬

山吧。

小王：好！

Xuemei: Xiao Wang, we've wanted to visit the Summer Palace for a long time. Thank you for coming here with us today.

Xiao Wang: Please don't mention it, you're too polite.

Xiaojie: Brother, there are so many entrances, which one should we go in?

Xiao Wang: This is called the East Palace Gate. It's the formal entrance for the Summer Palace. The middle of the entrance was reserved for the emperor and empress, there was no way other people could go in through here.

Xiaojie: Then how did they go in?

Xiao Wang: Only through the small gates at the two sides.

Xuemei: Who would have thought there would be so many rules even for gates? Let's go.

Xiaojie: This place is massive! Brother, which way should we go?

Xiao Wang: This way, follow me. Xiaojie, the Summer Palace might seem huge, with over three thousand rooms. But it's actually just made up of three parts.

Xiaojie: Which parts?

Xiao Wang: The Palace area, Longevity Hill and Kunming Lake. Which part would you like to see?

Xuemei: We want to see them all. But we don't know which one first.

Xiaojie: I want to see Palace area. Is that where the emperor used to live?

Xiao Wang: OK. The Palace area is where the Empress Dowager Cixi and the emperor attended to political affairs. You can even see the Empress Dowager's Qingong.

Xiaojie: Qingong? What's that?

Xiao Wang: Oh, "qin" means to sleep. Qingong is where the emperor and the Empress Dowager used to rest.

Xuemei: The Empress Dowager and the emperor lived at the Summer Palace as well? Didn't they live in the Forbidden City?

Xiaojie: They only came here occasionally for holidays, right?

Xiao Wang: Not really. The Empress Dowager liked staying here a lot, sometimes she'd stay for as long as half a year or more.

Xiaojie: Oh, I see.

Xuemei: This must be the famous Long Corridor? I've seen it many times on postcards.

Xiaojie: What are all these paintings? I don't understand them at all!

Xiao Wang: Even I don't understand some of them. These are landscape paintings of West Lake. Some are folk stories.

Xuemei: I think this Long Corridor is a good idea. It separates the mountain and lake, and it's a shelter against the wind and sun while you enjoy the sights.

Xiao Wang: You're spot on, that's exactly right.

Xiaojie: Mum, quick, come and have a look. This lake is so pretty!

Xiao Wang: This is Kunming Lake. It's shaped like a birthday peach, whereas the Longevity Hill behind it is shaped like a bat.

Xiaojie: Bat? Why a bat? How ugly!

Xiao Wang: Got you, huh? That's because the "fu" in "bianfu" sounds the same as the "fu" in "xingfu"or happiness.

Xuemei: So the design is for good luck.

Xiao Wang: That's certainly one consideration, but it's also a major feature of Chinese landscaped gardens.

Xiaojie: I don't get it. I don't get it. Let's go and climb the mountain.

Xiao Wang: OK!

生词

1.	正门	zhèng mén	名	formal entrance
2.	由……组成	yóu…zǔ chéng	动	be made up of
3.	部分	bù fen	名	part
4.	办公	bàn gōng	动	work
5.	寝宫	qǐn gōng	名	resting palace
6.	偶尔	ǒu ěr	副	occasionally
7.	著名	zhù míng	形	famous
8.	长廊	cháng láng	名	long corridor
9.	画	huà	动	draw
10.	设计	shè jì	动	design
11.	分隔	fēn gé	动	separate
12.	点子	diǎn zi	名	idea
13.	形状	xíng zhuàng	名	shape
14.	寿桃	shòu táo	名	birthday peach
15.	蝙蝠	biān fú	名	bat
16.	图	tú	动	pursue
17.	固然	gù rán	副	certainly
18.	反映	fǎn yìng	动	reflect

注释

1. 它是由三个部分组成的。

↪ 由 sth. 组成, to be made up of or comprised of something. For instance, 我们的节目由五个部分组成, our program is made up of five sections, or five parts.

2. 他们不是偶尔来这里度假的吧?

↪ They only came here occasionally, didn't they? 偶尔 means occasionally, or once in a while.

3. 有时候她一住就是大半年呢。

↪ Sometimes she would live here more than half the year. 大半年 means more than half the year. 小半年 would mean less than half the year.

4. 它的形状看起来像个寿桃。

↪ Imperial Chinese architecture is full of symbolic meanings. For example, Kunming Lake, which is man-made, is shaped like a 寿桃, a longevity peach. This comes from a traditional fable about how you can attain immortality by eating these special peaches from heaven. Note that we usually don't put the 儿 ending on 寿桃. You can actually buy peaches like this in a marketplace, but they are not real fruit. They are made from pastry.

5. 而后边的万寿山呢，它的形状像一只蝙蝠。

↪ Longevity Mountain behind the lake looks just like a bat, 蝙蝠. But why is that considered auspicious? Well, the character 蝠, from 蝙蝠, sounds just like the 福 as in 幸福. They are written differently, but the characters are pronounced the same way. So, bats are considered a symbol of good fortune.

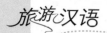

Old Summer Palace

There are actually two summer palaces around Beijing, one built after the other. The older one dates from the 18th century, when Emperor Qianlong created the Garden of Perfect Purity, 圆明园. In English, we just call this the Old Summer Palace. Besides a spectacular landscape garden, it also housed buildings in various european styles. This was built at the height of the Qing Dynasty when the emperor specifically wanted to include samples of architectural styles from around the world. Later, during the Opium Wars in 1860 this palace was stormed by western troops, who destroyed the palaces and removed the treasures. The ruins of the central water fountain, originally one of the most spectacular sites, have become an important symbol of foreign aggression in China. Many people believe these ruins should be kept as they are, as a potent reminder of China's history.

Empress Dowager Cixi set about establishing a new Summer Palace in 1888 to replace the old one. This palace is called 颐和园 in Chinese, and is located only a kilometre or two from the Old Summer Palace.

语言点

偶尔 occasionally

我一般在家吃饭，偶尔也会出去吃。

I normally eat at home, but occasionally I go out to eat as well.

句型 及 替换练习

1. 由……组成 be made up of

这个旅行团由三个国家的旅客组成。

This tour group is made up of tourists from three countries.

替换例句：

这间公寓由四个房间组成。

颐和园大概由三个部分组成。

2. 不知（道）……（才）好 to not know what to do

他不明白我的意思，我真不知道怎么说才好。

He doesn't understand what I mean. I really don't know what to say.

替换例句：

他第一次去女朋友家，紧张得不知该说什么好。

今天点的菜全是她爱吃的，她都不知道要先吃哪一个才好。

3. 固然……不过…… admitting A, but B

工作固然重要，不过也要注意休息。

Work is important, but we have to pay attention to rest.

替换例句：

坐飞机旅游固然方便，不过票价可比火车票贵多了。

烤鸭固然好吃，不过经常吃会让人变胖的。

第 *13* 课

包饺子
Make
Dumplings

课文

Biǎo jiě
表 姐
　　　　Nǐ hǎo　Hǎo jiǔ bú jiàn
Péng you：你好！好久不见。
朋 友

Biǎo jiě　Zhè shì wǒ biǎo dì de hái zi　jiào Xiǎo jié　Xiǎo
表 姐：这是我表弟的孩子，叫 小 杰。 小

　　　　jié　zhè shì Wáng ā yí
　　　　杰，这是 王 阿姨。

Xiǎo jié　Ā yí hǎo
小 杰：阿姨好！

Péng you　Zhè hái zi zhēn piào liang　lái　lǐ bian qǐng
朋 友：这孩子真 漂 亮，来，里边 请 。

Xiǎo jié　Gū gu　Xiǎo Wáng ā yí de jiā zhēn bù cuò　gēn wǒ
小 杰：姑姑，小 王 阿姨的家 真 不错， 跟我

men jiā wán quán bù yí yàng
们 家 完 全 不 一 样 。

Biǎo jiě　Wáng jiě　nǐ kàn xiàn zài de hái zi　gēn běn jiù gǎo
表 姐：王 姐，你 看 现 在 的 孩 子，根 本 就 搞

bù qīng chu zhù sì hé yuàn shì yì zhǒng shén me yàng
不 清 楚 住 四 合 院 是 一 种 什 么 样

de gǎn jué
的 感 觉 。

Péng you　Shì a　wǒ men xiǎo de shí hou　duō yǒu yì si
朋 友：是 啊，我 们 小 的 时 候，多 有 意 思

a　　Xià tiān zhuō zhuo qū qur　　dōng tiān duī dui
啊 。 夏 天 捉 捉 蛐 蛐 儿，冬 天 堆 堆

xuě rénr　　shuí jiā zuò le hào chī de cài　wǒ men
雪 人 儿，谁 家 做 了 好 吃 的 菜，我 们

dōu dà jiā yì qǐ qù chī　yì qǐ qù fēn xiǎng
都 大 家 一 起 去 吃，一 起 去 分 享 。

Biǎo jiě　Shì a　nà shí hou wǒ jiù tè xǐ huan dào nǐ men jiā
表 姐：是 啊，那 时 候 我 就 特 喜 欢 到 你 们 家

chī jiǎo zi　wǒ kě jì de nǐ men jiā de jiǎo zi tè
吃 饺 子，我 可 记 得 你 们 家 的 饺 子 特

hào chī
好 吃 。

Péng you　You　hái diàn ji zhe ne　jīn tiān wǒ jiù gěi nǐ men bāo
朋 友：呦，还 惦 记 着 呢，今 天 我 就 给 你 们 包

jiǎo zi chī
饺 子 吃 。

Xiǎo jié　Hǎo a　wǒ zuì xǐ huan chī jiǎo zi le　　Chūn
小 杰：好 啊，我 最 喜 欢 吃 饺 子 了 。 春

jié de shí hou　bà ba gěi wǒ hé mā ma zuò jiǎo
节 的 时 候，爸 爸 给 我 和 妈 妈 做 饺

zi chī
子 吃 。

Péng you　Shì ma　Lái　nǐ men zhè bian qǐng　wǒ gěi nǐ men
朋 友：是 吗？来，你 们 这 边 请，我 给 你 们

ná hǎo chī de qù
拿 好 吃 的 去。

Xiǎo jié　Gū gu　tā shì nǐ de lǎo péng you ma
小 杰：姑姑，她 是 你 的 老 朋 友 吗？

Biǎo jié　Shì a　wǒ men xiǎo shí hou hái shi lín jū ne
表 姐：是 啊，我 们 小 时 候 还 是 邻 居 呢。

Hòu lái tā qù le guó wài　suǒ yǐ gū gu yǒu hěn
后 来 她 去 了 国 外，所 以 姑 姑 有 很

cháng shí jiān dōu méi jiàn guo tā le
长 时 间 都 没 见 过 她 了。

Péng you　Lái　lái　zhè shì táng　huā shēng hé guā zǐ
朋 友：来，来，这 是 糖 、花 生 和 瓜 子，

nǐ men xiān chī zhe　wǒ qù gěi nǐ men bāo jiǎo
你 们 先 吃 着，我 去 给 你 们 包 饺

zi qù
子 去。

Xiǎo jié　Ā yí　wǒ gēn nǐ yì qǐ qù bāo jiǎo zi ba
小 杰：阿 姨，我 跟 你 一 起 去 包 饺 子 吧。

Péng you　O　Nǐ huì bāo ma
朋 友：哦？你 会 包 吗？

Xiǎo jié　Wǒ bú huì　dàn shì wǒ kě yǐ xué a
小 杰：我 不 会，但 是 我 可 以 学 啊。

Biǎo jié　Nà jiù yì qǐ bāo ba　zì jǐ bāo de chī zhe
表 姐：那 就 一 起 包 吧，自 己 包 的 吃 着

gèng xiāng
更 香。

Biǎo jié　You　méi zhàn qǐ lai　Méi guān xi　zài shì
表 姐：呦，没 站 起 来。没 关 系，再 试

yí gè
一 个。

Xiǎo jié　Wǒ jué de zhè ge jiǎo zi de xíng zhuàng hǎo xiàng
小 杰：我 觉 得 这 个 饺 子 的 形 状 好 像

ěr duo yí yàng
耳朵一样。

Péng you　Nǐ hái bié shuō　lǎo rén guò qù jiù cháng shuō　dào
朋　友：你还别说，老人过去就常说，到

le dōng tiān chī le jiǎo zi　ěr duo jiù bù róng yì bèi
了冬天吃了饺子，耳朵就不容易被

dòng shāng
冻伤。

Xiǎo jié　Suǒ yǐ cái zhǎng de xiàng ěr duo a
小杰：所以才长得像耳朵啊。

Péng you　Lái　Xiǎo jié　duō chī diǎnr　Dāng xīn tàng
朋　友：来，小杰，多吃点儿。当心烫！

Xiǎo jié　Yi　zhè ge jiǎo zi li zěn me yǒu yì kē táng a
小杰：咦，这个饺子里怎么有一颗糖啊？

Biǎo jié　Zhè shì Wáng ā yí tè yì gěi nǐ bāo de　xī wàng nǐ
表姐：这是王阿姨特意给你包的，希望你

yǐ hòu de shēng huó a　tián tián mì mì
以后的生活啊，甜甜蜜蜜。

Xiǎo jié　Zhēn yǒu yì si　yuán lái táng yě kě yǐ dāng
小杰：真有意思，原来糖也可以当

xiànr
馅儿。

Biǎo jié　Bù guāng shì táng　guò Chūn jié de shí hou　hái yǒu rén
表姐：不光是糖，过春节的时候，还有人

wǎng jiǎo zi li bāo yìng bì ne
往饺子里包硬币呢。

Xiǎo jié　Yìng bì　Nà zěn me chī a　Duō zāng a
小杰：硬币？那怎么吃啊？多脏啊！

Péng you　Bìng bú shì zhēn de chī　Bú guò dào le Chūn jié de
朋　友：并不是真的吃。不过到了春节的

shí hou nǐ yào zhēn shi chī dào zhè yàng de jiǎo zi　jiù
时候你要真是吃到这样的饺子，就

143

yí dìng huì yǒu fú qi   hái huì zhèng dào qián de
一 定 会 有 福气，还 会 挣 到 钱 的。

Xiǎo jié   Shì zhēn de ma   Ā yí   nǐ jīn tiān zuò le nà zhǒng
小 杰：是 真 的 吗？阿姨，你 今 天 做 了 那 种

jiǎo zi ma   Wǒ lái zhǎo zhao kàn
饺 子 吗？我 来 找 找 看。

Cousin/Friend: Hello. Haven't seen you for a long time.

Cousin: This is my cousin's daughter, Xiaojie. Xiaojie, this is aunt Wang.

Xiaojie: Hello aunt Wang!

Friend: Such a pretty girl! Come on. Please come inside.

Xiaojie: Aunt, aunt Wang's courtyard is really interesting; it's totally different from my house.

Cousin: Ms. Wang, the kids today have no idea what it's like to live in a square courtyard.

Friend: Yes, what fun we had when we were little. We'd catch crickets in summer, make snowmen in winter, and if anyone had made something nice to eat, we'd all share it.

Cousin: Yes, even back then I loved coming to your house for dumplings. I remember your dumplings were especially tasty.

Friend: Haha, you still remember. Great! Well today I'll make dumplings for you.

Xiaojie: Great! I love dumplings. At Chinese New Year, dad makes dumplings for my mum and me.

Friend: Really? Come here, I'll go and get something for you.

Xiaojie: Aunt, is she an old friend of yours?

Cousin: Yes, we used to be neighbours when we were kids. Later she went overseas, so your aunt hasn't seen her for a long time.

Friend: Here's some candy, peanuts and sunflower seeds. Help yourselves. I'll go and make dumplings for you.

Xiaojie: Auntie, let me help you make them.

Friend: Oh? Do you know how?

Xiaojie: No, but I want to learn.

Cousin: Then let's make them together. They taste better when you make them yourselves.

Cousin: It falls flat. That's alright. Try another one.

Xiaojie: I think dumplings are shaped like ears.

Friend: Right. The older folks used to say, if you eat dumplings, your ears won't get frostbite easily in winter.

Xiaojie: That's why they look like ears.

Friend: Come on, Xiaojie, eat up. But be careful. They're hot!

Xiaojie: Hey, this dumpling has a sweet inside.

Cousin: Aunt Wang put it in specially, hoping your future will be sweet like candy.

Xiaojie: That's interesting. Sweets can make a filling too.

Cousin: Not just sweets. During Chinese New Year, some people put coins in dumplings.

Xiaojie: Coins? How do you eat them? How dirty!

Friend: You don't really eat them. But if you get one of these dumplings during Chinese New Year, it means you'll have a lucky year and make lots of money.

Xiaojie: Is that for real? Auntie, did you make one of these dumplings today? Let me try to find one.

生词

1.	捉	zhuō	动	catch
2.	蛐蛐儿	qū qūr	名	cricket
3.	堆	duī	动	pile up
4.	雪人儿	xuě rénr	名	snowman
5.	分享	fēn xiǎng	动	share
6.	惦记	diàn jì	动	worry about
7.	春节	Chūn jiē	名	Spring Festival
8.	邻居	lín jū	名	neighbour
9.	糖	táng	名	candy
10.	花生	huā shēng	名	peanut
11.	瓜子	guā zǐ	名	sunflower seed
12.	香	xiāng	形	fragrant, tasty
13.	耳朵	ěr duo	名	ear
14.	冻	dòng	动	freeze
15.	特意	tè yì	副	especially
16.	甜甜蜜蜜	tián tián mì mì	形	sweet
17.	馅儿	xiànr	名	filling
18.	硬币	yìng bì	名	coin
19.	脏	zāng	形	dirty
20.	福气	fú qi	名	good luck

注释

1. 根本就搞不清楚住四合院是一种什么样的感觉。
- They don't have a clue what it's like to live in a courtyard home. 搞不清楚, to not be able to figure something out. 清楚 is clear, understandable. 搞清楚 is like "get to the bottom of something", "to figure it out".

2. 还惦记着呢。
- 惦记 is to remember something fondly, to long for something. So today they're going to make and eat *jiaozi* together. 包 is the verb used for making *jiaozi*, which literally means to wrap them, 包饺子.

3. 自己包的吃着更香。
- The ones you make yourself are much more tasty. 更好吃, or as they say here, 吃着更香. 香 usually means fragrant, but here we would say tasty in English.

4. 这个饺子的形状好像耳朵一样。
- The shape, 形状, of this *jiaozi* looks like an ear.

5. 你还别说，老人过去就常说，到了冬天吃了饺子，耳朵就不容易被冻伤。
- 你还别说, this is a colloquial term to indicate that you are reminded of something, or that there is some truth in whatever has just been said, even if it was just a joke.

6. 到了春节的时候你要真是吃到这样的饺子，就一定会有福气。
- In China it's felt that if you are lucky enough to discover a coin inside your *jiaozi* during Spring Festival, then you will have good luck, 福气, all year.

文化
背景

Dumpling

A wide variety of different Chinese foods fall under the English term "dumpling". Of these, 饺子 are the most popular in northern China, where they are seen as a symbol of festivity and are served as the main dish during Spring Festival celebrations. In vast areas of north China, especially in the countryside, *jiaozi* are served throughout the year, and especially when there are guests for dinner. As we will discuss in a future lesson, some places even offer what is called a 饺子宴, literally a *jiaozi* banquet, where you are treated to a sampling of dozens of different types of *jiaozi*, boiled, steamed, fried, roasted, and containing an unlimited variety of fillings.

Jiaozi are made with a thin pastry wrapper, usually with seasoned mincemeat as the filling. They are usually in the shape of crescent moon, or, as some say, in the shape of ears. This led to the tradition that *jiaozi* should be eaten in winter to help avoid frostbite on the ears. *Jiaozi* are normally boiled, but can also be steamed under cover. Steamed *jiaozi* are what we call 蒸饺.

A great variety of food can be used for the filling. Minced pork, mutton and beef as well as prawn or shrimp are common meats. These are then combined with various vegetables and dried mushrooms.

After cooking, the *jiaozi* are commonly dipped in a sauce of vinegar and soy sauce. Again, there are many variations to the dipping sauce depending on the local custom.

In southern China, another style of dumplings are called 馄饨. In English we refer to these as wontons, from the Cantonese pronunciation. Wontons are similar to *jiaozi*, but have a thinner wrapping and contain less filling. Wontons are also folded in a different way that leaves a loose flap, and they are always boiled and served in a broth.

In 1969, a Tang Dynasty tomb was excavated in Xinjiang, where a wooden bowl was unearthed containing a number of dumplings, looking just like the *jiaozi* of today. This indicates that *jiaozi* have been enjoyed in China for at least 1000 years.

1. V+不清楚 the result of the verb is not clear

他一直搞不清楚出发时间。

He could never quite figure out the departure time.

2. 惦记 remember fondly, miss, worry

妈妈一直很惦记去国外留学的女儿。

The mother always missed her daughter who had gone to study abroad.

你还别说…… show agreement

你还别说，他说的还挺有道理的。

You know, he actually said something quite reasonable.

替换例句：

你还别说，他唱起歌来还真像个明星。

你还别说，他修起电脑来还真有两下子。

第 *14* 课

北海公园
Beihai Park

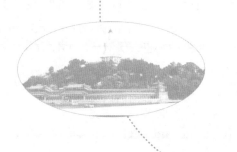

课文

小杰：<ruby>爸爸<rt>Bà ba</rt></ruby>，<ruby>快<rt>kuài</rt></ruby><ruby>点儿<rt>diǎnr</rt></ruby><ruby>啊<rt>a</rt></ruby>。<ruby>快<rt>Kuài</rt></ruby><ruby>到<rt>dào</rt></ruby><ruby>我<rt>wǒ</rt></ruby><ruby>这<rt>zhè</rt></ruby><ruby>边<rt>bian</rt></ruby><ruby>来<rt>lái</rt></ruby>。

Xiǎo jié　爸爸，快点儿啊。快到我这边来。

黄人豪：来了。这个地方一点儿都没变啊，

Huáng Rén háo　Lái le　Zhè ge dì fang yì diǎnr dōu méi biàn a

白塔、绿树、红墙，我仿佛又回

bái tǎ　lù shù　hóng qiáng　wǒ fǎng fú yòu huí

到了以前的生活。

dào le yǐ qián de shēng huó

小杰：爸爸，你以前经常来这儿吗？

Xiǎo jié　Bà ba　nǐ yǐ qián jīng cháng lái zhèr ma

黄人豪：那当然了。爸爸小的时候就经常

Huáng Rén háo　Nà dāng rán le　Bà ba xiǎo de shí hou jiù jīng cháng

到这儿来划船。

dào zhèr lái huá chuán

小杰：是吗？那个时候就有北海公园了？
Xiǎo jié：Shì ma？Nà ge shí hou jiù yǒu Běi hǎi Gōng yuán le？

黄人豪：看你说的，这个地方有近一千年
Huáng Rén háo：Kàn nǐ shuō de，zhè ge dì fang yǒu jìn yì qiān nián
的历史了，不过当时它是皇帝一个
de lì shǐ le，bú guò dāng shí tā shì huáng dì yí ge
人的花园。别人是不能进来的。
rén de huā yuán。Bié rén shì bù néng jìn lái de。

小杰：唉，那多没劲啊，我就爱和很多同
Xiǎo jié：Ai，nà duō méi jìn a，wǒ jiù ài hé hěn duō tóng
学一起玩儿。
xué yì qǐ wánr。

小杰：爸爸，一、二、三……刻着九条龙的
Xiǎo jié：Bà ba，yī、èr、sān……kè zhe jiǔ tiáo lóng de
墙。我上次和妈妈去故宫的时
qiáng。Wǒ shàng cì hé mā ma qù Gù gōng de shí
候好像也看过这样的墙。
hou hǎo xiàng yě kàn guo zhè yàng de qiáng。

黄人豪：对，这叫九龙壁。故宫的那个也叫
Huáng Rén háo：Duì，zhè jiào Jiǔ lóng bì。Gù gōng de nà ge yě jiào
九龙壁。
Jiǔ lóng bì。

小杰：嗯，妈妈说中国古代的皇帝都喜
Xiǎo jié：Ng，mā ma shuō Zhōng guó gǔ dài de huáng dì dōu xǐ
欢龙，是这样的吗？那为什么一
huan lóng，shì zhè yàng de ma？Nà wèi shén me yí
定要刻上九条龙呢？
dìng yào kè shàng jiǔ tiáo lóng ne？

黄人豪：小杰，龙在中国一直被看作是
Huáng Rén háo：Xiǎo jié，lóng zài Zhōng guó yì zhí bèi kàn zuò shì
皇帝的象征。九龙不仅代表皇
huáng dì de xiàng zhēng。Jiǔ lóng bù jǐn dài biǎo huáng

dì de zūn guì　　gèng yǒu rén rèn wéi tā huì gěi zhěng
帝的尊贵，更有人认为它会给整

gè guó jiā dài lái jí xiáng de
个国家带来吉祥的。

Xiǎo jié　Ai　bà ba　nǐ kàn　jiǔ tiáo lóng de yán sè dōu bù
小　杰：哎，爸爸，你看，九条龙的颜色都不

yí yàng　zhēn hǎo kàn
一样，真好看。

Huáng Rén háo　Shì a
黄　人豪：是啊。

Xiǎo jié　Bà ba　nǐ kàn zhè bian de fēng jǐng zhēn hǎo　Nǐ kàn　nà
小　杰：爸爸，你看这边的风景真好。你看，那

bian yǒu rén zài huá chuán　wǒ men yě qù ba
边有人在划船，我们也去吧。

Huáng Rén háo　Xiǎo jié　wǒ men xiē yí huìr　zài qù huá ba
黄　人豪：小杰，我们歇一会儿再去划吧。

Bà ba gāng cái yì kǒu qì zǒu le zhè me jiǔ　yǒu diǎnr
爸爸刚才一口气走了这么久，有点儿

lèi le
累了。

Xiǎo jié　Bà ba　kuài zǒu　kuài zǒu　wǒ lái huá chuán　nǐ
小　杰：爸爸，快走，快走，我来划船，你

zuò zhe xiū xi hǎo le
坐着休息好了。

Huáng Rén háo　Ai　Xiǎo jié　yào bu rán wǒ xiān dài nǐ qù　Fǎng
黄　人豪：哎，小杰，要不然我先带你去"仿

shàn　chī diǎnr dōng xi ba
膳"吃点儿东西吧。

Xiǎo jié　Fǎng shàn　nà shì shén me dì fang
小　杰：仿膳，那是什么地方？

Huáng Rén háo　Xiǎo jié a　yǐ qián huáng dì chī fàn jiù jiào zuò yòng
黄　人豪：小杰啊，以前皇帝吃饭就叫作用

膳。"仿膳"是一个饭店的名字，

就在北海公园里头，卖的都是皇

帝以前吃的东西和一些宫廷小吃。

小杰：宫廷小吃？

黄人豪：对，就是以前皇宫里的人经常

吃的小吃。比如说豌豆黄、芸豆

卷、小窝头、肉末烧饼等等。

小杰：啊，别说了，我们先去吃吧。

黄人豪：你现在不着急划船了？

小杰：顾不上，我们先去吃好吃的

再说。

Xiaojie: Dad, hurry up. Come over here.

Huang Renhao: Coming. It hasn't changed here at all, the white tower, green trees, red walls. It's just like being back in the old days.

Xiaojie: Dad, did you use to come here often?

Huang Renhao: Sure. When I was little, I used to come here and row boats all the time.

Xiaojie: Really? Beihai Park was around back then?

Huang Renhao: Don't be silly, this place has almost one thousand years of history, although back then it was the emperor's personal garden. Ordinary people couldn't come in.

Xiaojie: Oh, that's no fun. I love hanging out with my friends.

Xiaojie: Dad, 1, 2, 3...the wall with nine dragons. I think I saw a wall like this last time when I went to the Forbidden City with mum.

Huang Renhao: Yes, this is called the Nine Dragon Wall. The one in the Forbidden City is also called the Nine Dragon Wall.

Xiaojie: Hmm, mum says the emperors in ancient China all liked dragons. Is that true? Then why do they have to have nine dragons engraved on them?

Huang Renhao: Dragons have always symbolized the emperor in China. Nine dragons not only show the power of the emperor, and some people believed they would bring luck to the whole nation.

Xiaojie: Look, dad, the nine dragons all have different colours. They look great.

Huang Renhao: Really.

Xiaojie: Dad, the view here is so beautiful. Look, people are rowing boats over there. Let's go too.

Huang Renhao: Let's take a break first. I'm a bit tired from all that walking.

Xiaojie: Dad, come on, let's go, I'll row. You can sit there and rest.

Huang Renhao: Hey, Xiaojie, how about I take you to eat at "Fangshan"?

Xiaojie: Fangshan, what kind of place is that?

Huang Renhao: In the old days when the emperor dined, it was called "yong shan". "Fangshan" is the name of a restaurant in Beihai Park. Supposedly they serve what the emperor used to eat and some imperial snacks.

Xiaojie: Imperial snacks?

Huang Renhao: That's right, snacks that people used to eat in the palace. Like pea flour cake, bean rolls, mini buns, mince stuffed sesame pancakes…

Xiaojie: Oh, please stop. Let's go there now.

Huang Renhao: So you're not in a hurry to go boating?

Xiaojie: Not yet. Let's go and eat some yummy stuff first.

1.	仿佛	fǎng fú	副	as if
2.	划船	huá chuán	动	row a boat
3.	花园	huā yuán	名	park, garden
4.	刻	kè	动	engrave
5.	墙	qiáng	名	wall
6.	古代	gǔ dài	名	ancient times
7.	看作	kàn zuò	动	look upon as
8.	象征	xiàng zhēng	名	symbol
9.	尊贵	zūn guì	名	dignity
10.	认为	rèn wéi	动	think, believe
11.	吉祥	jí xiáng	形	lucky, auspicious
12.	叫作	jiào zuò	动	be called

注释

1．经常到这儿来划船。
- Here, 划 is pronounced in the 2nd tone, meaning to row. This character is sometimes pronounced in the 4th tone, 划, as in 计划, a plan. 划船 is to row a boat.

2．九龙壁
- They come to the Nine Dragon Wall or Screen, 九龙壁. This is one of the main sites within the park area. 壁 is a wall, 墙壁.

3．龙在中国一直被看作是皇帝的象征。
- 被看作 is to be seen as, to be thought of as being something.

4．我们歇一会儿再去划吧。
- 歇 is a colloquial term for 休息, to rest.

5．爸爸刚才一口气走了这么久。
- 一口气 literally means in one breath, but it's used figuratively to indicate that something has been done without stopping, without interruption.

6．要不然我先带你去"仿膳"吃点儿东西吧。
- 要不然 literally means otherwise. Here it's used to make a suggestion. 仿膳 is one of the most famous old restaurants in Beijing. 膳 refers to 御膳, a fancy term to refer to the emperor's meals. 膳 means meal, for example, 用膳 is to eat a meal. 仿 is to imitate, so 仿膳, just like the emperor's meals. This restaurant is located on the site of what was once one of the imperial kitchens, and they serve imperial style food.

7．顾不上
- 顾不上 means to not be able to pay attention to something, to not have time for that.

Beihai Park

Beihai Park has been a playground for emperors for hundreds of years. Some attribute this site to Kublai Khan, grandson of Genghis Khan and founder of the Yuan Dynasty in China. The island at the southern end of the lake is said to have been created by excavating the site on the orders of Kublai Khan, and this location is associated with his grand palace. This would have been the centre of Beijing before the Forbidden city was built in the Ming and Qing dynasties. Unfortunately, all that remains of the Khan's palace today is a large jar made of green jade.

Dominating in this island, known as the Jade Islet, is a 36m high white dagoba, originally built in 1651 and then rebuilt in 1741. This is one of the most famous dagobas in all of China.

Stupas of all kinds appeared in China with the import of Buddhism. In Chinese, these are known as 塔, including all styles of stupas and pagodas. Initially, stupas were said to contain some sort of Buddhist relic or ashes of a saintly Buddha. Other times, stupas were built to safekeep holy scriptures and various ritual implements. This leads to the terms 佛塔, Buddha's pagoda, or 宝塔, treasure pagoda.

The dagoba is a pagoda of Tibetan style and is sometimes called 喇嘛塔, after the Lamanist school of Buddhism. Mongolians have also been followers of this school, which originated in Tibet. So it makes sense that Kublai Khan would set about building a large dagoba in Beijing after selecting the city as the capital of the Yuan Dynasty. It was hoped that the dagoba would symbolize the regime's divine power and keep the nation at peace.

Another attraction in Beihai Park is the Nine-Dragon Wall 九龙壁, sculpted in nine colours of glazed tile. Screen walls were common in traditional architecture for giving privacy to an entrance as well as serving as a symbol of rank. The number nine and the dragon are both symbols of the emperor. The screen wall in Beihai Park is considered the most splendid of three similar walls in China dating from the Ming Dynasty. So the wall in Beihai Park is definitely worth seeing when you visit.

语言点

1. 仿佛 as if

看着这些老照片，我仿佛又回到了从前。

Looking at these old photos, it's as if I've gone back to the past.

2. 近 almost, up to

中国有近五千年的文化历史。

China has almost five thousand years of cultural history.

句型 及 替换练习

1. 一口气 the action happens continuously

他太渴了，一口气喝掉了一整瓶的水。

He was too thirsty. He drank a whole bottle of water at once.

替换例句：

他饿极了，居然一口气吃了三十个饺子。

这本书我是一口气读完的。

2. 顾不上 can't pay attention to

他一工作起来就什么都忘了，常常连晚饭都顾不上吃。

When he starts working, he forgets everything else. He often even forgets to eat dinner.

替换例句：

他光顾着照相，连话都顾不上和我们说了。

他整天工作，都顾不上回家了。

第 *15* 课

胡同
Hutong

课文

Hutong

Xuě méi 　Wǒ men jīn tiān zǒu le zhè me cháng shí jiān　wǒ dōu
雪 梅：我 们 今 天 走 了 这 么 长 时 间，我 都
kuài lèi sǐ le
快 累 死 了。

Tóng shì 　Nà wǒ men dào qián bian zuò huìr　zài zǒu ba
同 事：那 我 们 到 前 边 坐 会儿 再 走 吧。

Xuě méi 　Hǎo de　 Kàn 　wǒ mǎi le yì běn jiè shào Zhōng guó
雪 梅：好 的。看，我 买 了 一 本 介 绍 中 国
jiàn zhù de shū 　bú cuò ba
建 筑 的 书，不 错 吧。

Tóng shì 　Wǒ kàn kan 　zhēn bú cuò 　hái yǒu hǎo duō tú
同 事：我 看 看，真 不 错，还 有 好 多 图
piàn ne
片 呢。

雪梅：你看，四合院，我一直对这种建
筑很感兴趣，你以前住过四合
院吗？

同事：没有，我们家以前一直住在楼
房里，不过我有朋友就住在四合
院里。

雪梅：说到四合院，我还想起一件有意思
的事情来呢。

同事：什么事情啊？看把你乐的。

雪梅：我刚到中国的时候，有一天闲着
没事儿，觉得闷得慌，我就顺路溜
达到一个小胡同去了。

同事：那里边很窄吧？

雪梅：没错，里边有一个院子，开着门，我
就忍不住走进去看看。

同事：真的吗？有人撵你吗？

雪梅：没有，不过里边出来了一个人

wèn wǒ nín zhǎo shuí xià de wǒ gǎn jǐn liū diào le
问 我，您 找 谁，吓 得 我 赶 紧 溜 掉 了。

Tóng shì　Ha ha pèng le ge dīng zi ba
同 事：哈 哈，碰 了 个 钉 子 吧。

Xuě méi　Zhè wǒ dào bú zài hu zhǐ kě xī wǒ méi yǒu jī
雪 梅：这 我 倒 不 在 乎，只 可 惜 我 没 有 机

huì hǎo hao kàn kan nà ge yuàn zi
会 好 好 看 看 那 个 院 子。

Tóng shì　Nǐ zhè me gǎn xìng qù de huà bù rú wǒ dài nǐ
同 事：你 这 么 感 兴 趣 的 话，不 如 我 带 你

qù ge dì fang kàn kan hǎo le
去 个 地 方 看 看 好 了。

Xuě méi　Nà tài hǎo le
雪 梅：那 太 好 了。

Tóng shì　Wǒ shuō de dì fang lí zhèr dǎo bù yuǎn yào bù wǒ
同 事：我 说 的 地 方 离 这 儿 倒 不 远，要 不 我

men xiàn zài jiù guò qu kàn kan
们 现 在 就 过 去 看 看？

Xuě méi　Hǎo wǒ men zǒu ba
雪 梅：好，我 们 走 吧。

Tóng shì　Xuě méi zhè jiù shì wǒ shuō de dì fang
同 事：雪 梅，这 就 是 我 说 的 地 方。

Xuě méi　Zhè li de hú tòng kě zhēn duō a wǒ men cóng nǎr
雪 梅：这 里 的 胡 同 可 真 多 啊，我 们 从 哪 儿

kāi shǐ a Wǒ de dǎo yóu xiǎo jiě
开 始 啊？我 的 导 游 小 姐？

Tóng shì　Ng sú huà shuō zhè Běi jīng a shì yǒu
同 事：嗯，俗 话 说，这 北 京 啊，是 有

míng de hú tòng sān qiān liù wú míng de hú tòng
名 的 胡 同 三 千 六，无 名 的 胡 同

sài niú máo
赛 牛 毛。

雪梅： Xuě méi　Ha ha　nǐ hái zhēn xiàng zhè me huí shìr
哈哈，你 还 真 像 这 么 回 事儿。

同事： Tóng shì　Wǎng zhèr zǒu　Zhè xiē dōu shì sì hé yuàn
往 这儿 走。这 些 都 是 四 合 院。

雪梅： Xuě méi　Zán men zǒu jìn diǎnr kàn kan
咱 们 走 近 点儿 看 看。

同事： Tóng shì　Hǎo a
好 啊！

雪梅： Xuě méi　Zhè ge shì mén dūnr ma
这 个 是 门 墩儿 吗？

同事： Tóng shì　Duì　bù tóng de mén dūnr jiù yǒu bù tóng de yì
对，不 同 的 门 墩儿 就 有 不 同 的 意
si　nǐ cóng mén dūnr jiù kě yǐ zhī dào zhè jiā rén
思，你 从 门 墩儿 就 可 以 知 道 这 家 人
shì zuò shén me gōng zuò de
是 做 什 么 工 作 的。

雪梅： Xuě méi　O　yuán lái shì zhè yàng de
哦，原 来 是 这 样 的。

同事： Tóng shì　zǒu　zán men jìn qu kàn kan
走，咱 们 进 去 看 看

雪梅： Xuě méi　Hǎo　Nà　yí ge sì hé yuàn li kě yǐ zhù sì jiā
好！那，一 个 四 合 院 里 可 以 住 四 家
rén ma
人 吗？

同事： Tóng shì　Nà kě bù yí dìng　yuán lái yǒu qián de rén shì yì jiā
那 可 不 一 定，原 来 有 钱 的 人 是 一 家
rén zhù yí ge huò zhě jǐ ge sì hé yuàn　méi qián de
人 住 一 个 或 者 几 个 四 合 院，没 钱 的
rén ne　shì hěn duō jiā rén hé zhù yí ge sì hé yuàn
人 呢，是 很 多 家 人 合 住 一 个 四 合 院。

雪梅： Xuě méi　Nà zhèr de sì hé yuàn hái hé yǐ qián yí yàng ma
那 这儿 的 四 合 院 还 和 以 前 一 样 吗？

Tóng shì　Bù　yǐ jing yǒu hěn dà bù tóng le　dà bù fen sì hé
同　事：不，已经有很大不同了，大部分四合

yuàn de gé jú dōu yǐ jing gǎi biàn le
　　　院的格局都已经改变了。

Xuě méi　Nǐ kàn　nàr　hái yǒu kōng tiáo　wǒ jué de sì
雪　梅：你看，那儿还有空调，我觉得四

hé yuàn de shēng huó yě biàn de xiàn dài huà le
　　　合院的生活也变得现代化了。

Tóng shì　Zài wǒ kàn lái　zhèr　wú lùn zěn me biàn　dōu
同　事：在我看来，这儿无论怎么变，都

shì Běi jīng shēng huó zuì zhòng yào de dài biǎo
　　　是北京生活最重要的代表。

Xuemei: We went a long walk today. I'm exhausted.

Colleague: Let's take a rest over there.

Xuemei: OK. Look, I bought a book on Chinese architecture. Pretty good, huh?

Colleague: Let me see. It's really good. There are lots of pictures inside.

Xuemei: Look at the square courtyard, I've always been interested in this sort of architecture. Have you lived in square courtyards before?

Colleague: No, we always lived in high-rise buildings, but I have friends who live in square courtyards.

Xuemei: Speaking of square courtyards, I just remembered something interesting.

Colleague: What's so funny?

Xuemei: When I first came to China, I had nothing to do one day and was bored, so I strolled into a little hutong.

Colleague: It must have been very narrow inside, right?

Xuemei: That's right. There was a yard inside, with the door open. I couldn't help but go in and have a look.

Colleague: Really? No one came to shoo you away?

Xuemei: No, but somebody did come out and ask me who I was

looking for. I left in a hurry.

Colleague: Haha, you got snubbed.

Xuemei: That's all right. It's just a pity I didn't get to have a proper look at the courtyard.

Colleague: Since you're so interested, how about I take you to a place to have a look?

Xuemei: That would be wonderful.

Colleague: The place I'm talking about isn't far from here. How about we head over there now?

Xuemei: OK, let's go.

Colleague: Xuemei, this is the place I was talking about.

Xuemei: There are so many hutongs here. Where do we start, Miss Tourguide?

Colleague: Hmm, the saying goes, Beijing has three thousand six hundred hutongs; there are more nameless hutongs than a bull's hairs.

Xuemei: Haha, you're really getting into the spirit.

Colleague: Xuemei, go this way. Look, these are all square courtyards.

Xuemei: Let's take a closer look.

Colleague: OK.

Xuemei: Hey, is this a doorstop?

Colleague: Yes, different doorstops mean different things. You can tell from the doorstop what sort of work the family did.

Xuemei: Oh, I see.

Colleague: Let's go and take a look inside.

Xuemei: Does a square courtyard accommodate four families?

Colleague: Not necessarily. In the old days wealthy families would live in one or more square courtyards. The people who weren't so well-off shared a square courtyard.

Xuemei: Are the square courtyards here like the ones before?

Colleague: No, they're vastly different now. Most square courtyards have changed their layouts.

Xuemei: Look, there's even an air-conditioner. Looks like life in the square courtyards has been modernized too.

Colleague: To me, no matter how it changes, this is the most important

生词

1.	建筑	jiàn zhù	名	architecture
2.	图片	tú piàn	名	picture
3.	楼房	lóu fáng	名	building
4.	闲	xián	形	idle, unoccupied
5.	顺路	shùn lù	形	by the way
6.	溜达	liū da	动	go for a walk
7.	窄	zhǎi	形	narrow
8.	忍不住	rěn bú zhù		cannot help
9.	撵	niǎn	动	drive out
10.	钉子	dīng zi	名	nail
11.	在乎	zài hu	动	care about
12.	俗话	sú huà	名	common saying
13.	门墩	mén dūn	名	doorstop
14.	格局	gé jú	名	layout
15.	空调	kōng tiáo	名	air-conditioner
16.	现代化	xiàn dài huà	动	modernize

注释

1. 有一天闲着没事儿，觉得闷得慌。

⭕ 闲 is to be idle, unoccupied, to have nothing to do. 觉得闷得慌, this is a colloquial expression. The key word is 闷, to be bored, in low spirits.

2. 有人撵你吗？

⭕ 撵 is to drive out.

3. 吓得我赶紧溜掉了。

⭕ 溜, to stroll. But in this case, 溜掉 would be to get out, to walk away, to get out of there. 赶紧溜掉, to get out of there fast.

4. 碰了个钉子吧。

⭕ She hit a nail, meaning she ran into a problem.

5. 不如我带你去个地方看看好了。

⭕ 不如 is used to show an option, such as it would be better if I take you to see some place.

6. 有名的胡同三千六，无名的胡同赛牛毛。

⭕ 赛 is to compete with. Here, the number of hutongs can compete with the 牛毛, the number of hairs on a cow. That's an awful lot.

7. 在我看来，这儿无论怎么变，都是北京生活最重要的代表。

⭕ 在我看来 is used to express in my view. It's similar to 我认为, I think, or 要我说, if you ask me. 无论 is regardless of, no matter what.

Hutongs and Courtyard Homes

Let's talk a little bit more about hutongs in Beijing. As we explained earlier, these refer to the narrow alleyways in the older parts of Beijing that connect the 四合院, the courtyard homes. The hutongs date originally from the Yuan Dynasty, although at least one hutong can be dated back to the Liao Dynasty before that, that's over 900 years ago. It is estimated that there were approximately 6000 hutongs around 1950. Recent development has changed the face of many hutongs, but often the modern streets retain their historical names. For example, Goldfish Hutong, 金鱼胡同, is now a wide street and home to 5 star hotels, but it still retains its name as a hutong. Some of the most significant hutongs are now protected as cultural relics, and any modern development has to preserve the nature of the hutong.

These alleyways, the hutongs and the courtyard homes, 四合院, that they link and connect, form the physical basis for the traditional family life in Beijing. They also provide the structure for a harmonious neighbourhood. Often, several families would live together in one 四合院, one courtyard home, so the courtyard was a public space for all to share. Other times, several courtyard homes would share public facilities like washrooms and bath houses. The family has always been the foundation of society in China, but there is a saying in Beijing that 远亲不如近邻, distant relatives are not as important as close neighbours. So these neighbourhoods were vital in providing a living space that everyone could share.

Many people nowadays prefer living in the hutongs to the modern houses and high-rise apartments, even though the hutongs often do not have modern plumbing or even heating systems. After all, the hutongs and

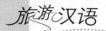

courtyard homes were built to reflect Chinese philosophy and *fengshui*, which is a Chinese term that is becoming much more common in the West. For example, most courtyard homes have their main entrance on the south side, so that you can 坐北朝南, sit in the north and face south, just as the emperor does in his palace. There are 门墩儿, as we learned in this lesson, to guard the entrance and a 屏风, a screen wall just inside the entrance to deflect evil spirits. Trees are planted in the courtyard to enhance the *qi* or the spiritual energy. Of course, these also have a very practical side. The screen or 屏风 also blocks the view from passers-by, and the trees provide shade for the summer. But in all, hutongs were designed as a comfortable place for families and neighbours to live, and at least some of that lifestyle still survives to this day.

语言点

1. 忍不住 can't resist

烤鸭太好吃了，虽然我害怕长胖，但还是忍不住多吃了几口。

Roast duck tastes too good. Although I'm afraid of gaining weight, I couldn't resist having a few extra bites.

2. 碰钉子 to run into a problem

求人帮忙要有礼貌，免得碰钉子。

When you ask someone for help, you should be polite. Otherwise, you might have a problem.

3. 或者 or

你明天或者后天来都行，我都有空儿。

You can come tomorrow or the day after tomorrow. I have time either day.

在……看来 in one's view

在我看来，到茶馆去看京剧很有意思。

In my view, watching Peking Opera at a teahouse is very interesting.

替换例句：

在我看来，中国菜很油腻。

在中国人看来，春节是一个很重要的日子。

第16课

什刹海
Shichahai
Lakes

课文

Huáng Rén háo　Jīn tiān tiān qì zhēn hǎo　　wǒ men yì jiā rén hǎo jiǔ
黄 人 豪：今 天 天 气 真 好 ，我 们 一 家 人 好 久

méi yǒu chū lái　wánr le ba
没 有 出 来 玩儿 了 吧 。

Xuě méi　Zhè li de fēng jǐng bú cuò　ér qiě kào jìn shuǐ biān
雪 梅：这 里 的 风 景 不 错 ，而 且 靠 近 水 边 ，

kōng qì yě hěn hǎo
空 气 也 很 好 。

Xiǎo jié　Bà ba　　wǒ men yí huìr zhǎo ge dì fang fàng fēng
小 杰：爸 爸 ，我 们 一 会儿 找 个 地 方 放 风

zheng ba
筝 吧 。

Huáng Rén háo　Xíng a　Xiǎo jié　nǐ bú shì yì zhí rāng rang yào kàn
黄 人 豪：行 啊 ，小 杰 ，你 不 是 一 直 嚷 嚷 要 看

Hòu hǎi ma　Zhè jiù shì
后 海 吗 ？ 这 就 是 。

Xiǎo jié　Shì ma　　Zhè yí piàn dōu shì Hòu hǎi ma
小　杰：是吗？这一片都是后海吗？

Huáng Rén háo　Lái　nǐ kàn　zhè jiù shì Yín dìng qiáo　Qiáo de
黄　人　豪：来，你看，这就是银锭桥。桥的

zhè bian shì Shí chà hǎi　yòu jiào Hòu hǎi　qiáo de
这边是什刹海，又叫后海，桥的

nà bian shì Qián hǎi
那边是前海。

Xuě méi　Zhè qiáo kě zhēn gòu xiù qi de
雪　梅：这桥可真够秀气的。

Huáng Rén háo　Nǐ bié kàn tā xiǎo　chuán shuō zhèr hái shì yì jǐng
黄　人　豪：你别看它小，传说这儿还是一景

ne　jiào Yín dìng guān shān　dōu shuō cóng zhèr
呢，叫银锭观山，都说从这儿

néng kàn dào Xī shān
能看到西山。

Xiǎo jié　Shì ma　Xī shān zài nǎr
小　杰：是吗？西山在哪儿？

Huáng Rén háo　Xiàn zài nǐ kàn bú dào le
黄　人　豪：现在你看不到了。

Xiǎo jié　Bà ba　wǒ jué de Běi jīng de dì míngr hěn qí guài
小　杰：爸爸，我觉得北京的地名儿很奇怪。

Huáng Rén háo　Wèi shén me ya
黄　人　豪：为什么呀？

Xiǎo jié　Běi hǎi ya　Shí chà hǎi ya　jiù shì yí ge hú
小　杰：北海呀，什刹海呀，就是一个湖，

wèi shén me yào jiào tā men　hǎi　ne
为什么要叫它们"海"呢？

Xuě méi　Wǒ yě jué de hěn qí guài　shì bú shì gǔ rén jué de
雪　梅：我也觉得很奇怪，是不是古人觉得

tā men tè bié dà　xiàng hǎi yáng shì de　jiù guǎn
它们特别大，像海洋似的，就管

tā men jiào hǎi le
它们叫海了？

黄 人 豪：你们都很善于发现问题，不过不
是这个意思。

小 杰：那是什么原因呢？

黄 人 豪：什刹海的"海"是"海子"的意思。

雪 梅：这两个词不是一个意思吗？

黄 人 豪：不，"海"是"海"，"海子"是"海
子"，海子在满语当中是湖泊的
意思。

小 杰：哦！原来是这样啊，爸爸你知道的
真多呀。

雪 梅：人豪，你看，这里还有很多酒吧，
到了晚上一定很热闹。

黄 人 豪：是啊，这儿既可以喝酒，又可以欣赏
美景，一举两得。

雪 梅：而且这里风景优美，闹中取静，
住在这儿也肯定不错。

黄 人 豪：对，历史上有很多名人都在这儿

zhù guo　　Qīng cháo jiù yǒu hǎo jǐ wèi wáng ye zhù zài
住 过 ，清 朝 就 有 好 几 位 王 爷 住 在

zhèr
这 儿 。

Xiǎo jié　　Wáng ye　Nà tā men de fáng zi xiàn zài hái zài ma
小 杰 ：王 爷 ？那 他 们 的 房 子 现 在 还 在 吗 ？

Huáng Rén háo　Yǒu a　　jiù ná Gōng wáng fǔ lái shuō ba　jiù bǎo
黄 人 豪 ：有 啊，就 拿 恭 王 府 来 说 吧，就 保

cún de hěn wán zhěng
存 得 很 完 整 。

Xuě méi　Chú le Gōng wáng fǔ　　hái yǒu qí tā de ma
雪 梅 ：除 了 恭 王 府，还 有 其 他 的 吗？

Huáng Rén háo　Hái yǒu Chún wáng fǔ　　hòu lái biàn chéng Sòng Qìng
黄 人 豪 ：还 有 醇 王 府，后 来 变 成 宋 庆

líng gù jū le
龄 故 居 了。

Xuě méi　Sòng Qìng líng　　Yě hěn yǒu míng ma
雪 梅 ：宋 庆 龄 ？也 很 有 名 嘛 。

Huáng Rén háo　Zhè Shí chà hǎi zhōu wéi a　kě yǐ shuō dào chù dōu
黄 人 豪 ：这 什 刹 海 周 围 啊，可 以 说 到 处 都

yǒu gù shi　　shuō shàng sān tiān sān yè dōu shuō
有 故 事， 说 上 三 天 三 夜 都 说

bù wán
不 完 。

Xiǎo jié　Dào chù　Zài nǎr ne
小 杰 ：到 处 ？在 哪 儿 呢 ？

Xuě méi　Xiǎo jié　Nǐ zài nàr zhē teng shén me ne
雪 梅 ：小 杰 ？你 在 那 儿 折 腾 什 么 呢 ？

Xiǎo jié　Zhǎo gù shi a
小 杰 ：找 故 事 啊 。

Huáng Rén háo　Ha ha　zǒu　yí huìr wǒ jiù dài nǐ men zhǎo gù
黄 人 豪 ：哈 哈，走， 一 会 儿 我 就 带 你 们 找 故

shi qù
事 去 。

Huang Renhao: It's a good day today. The family haven't gone out for sightseeing for a while.

Xuemei: The scenery here is beautiful and the air is fresh by the waterside.

Xiaojie: Dad, let's find a place to fly our kites.

Huang Renhao: OK. Xiaojie, this is the Houhai area you've always wanted to see.

Xiaojie: Yes? All this area is Houhai?

Huang Renhao: Come over here. You see, this is the Yinding Bridge. On this side of the bridge, it's Shichahai, also known as Houhai, and over there it's Qianhai.

Xuemei: This bridge is quite delicate.

Huang Renhao: It may be small, but it was a famous sight before, known as "Mountain Scene at the Yinding Bridge". It's said that you could see the West Hills from here.

Xiaojie: Really? Where are the West Hills?

Huang Renhao: You can't see them now.

Xiaojie: Dad, I find the place names in Beijng rather strange.

Huang Renhao: Why?

Xiaojie: Beihai, Shichahai, are they just lakes? Why call them seas?

Xuemei: I find the same. Could it be that people in ancient times thought that they were as big as a sea and named them seas afterwards?

Huang Renhao: You're good at finding problems. But that's not the reason.

Xiaojie: Then what is?

Huang Renhao: The "hai" in Shichahai is actually "haizi".

Xuemei: Don't these two words mean the same?

Huang Renhao: No. "Hai" is "sea", while "haizi" is not. "Haizi" is Manchu for lake.

Xiaojie: Oh, I see. You're really knowledgeable, dad.

Xuemei: Renhao, look, so many bars here. The nightlife here must be pretty lively.

Huang Renhao: Yeah. You can have a drink here and at the same time appreciate the beautiful scenery, killing two birds with one stone.

Xuemei: What's more, with the beautiful scenery, you can enjoy the solitude among all the excitement here. It must be a good place to live.

Huang Renhao: Right. Many celebrities lived here before in history. In the Qing Dynasty, even some princes lived here.

Xiaojie: Princes? Are their residences still around now?

Huang Renhao: Yes. Like Prince Gong's Mansion, it's well preserved.

Xuemei: Besides his, any others?

Huang Renhao: Prince Chun's Mansion is also around this area and is now the old residence of Song Qingling.

Xuemei: Song Qingling? That's a big name.

Huang Renhao: There are stories all around the Shichahai area. You could spend more than three days and three nights on them.

Xiaojie: All around? Where are they?

Xuemei: Xiaoijie, what are you looking around for?

Xiaojie: Stories.

Huang Renhao: Haha. Let's go and find some stories.

185

1.	天气	tiān qì	名	weather
2.	靠近	kào jìn	动	be close to
3.	嚷嚷	rāngrang	动	shout
4.	秀气	xiù qi	形	delicate
5.	奇怪	qí guài	形	strange
6.	古人	gǔ rén	名	ancient people
7.	海洋	hǎi yáng	名	sea
8.	善于	shàn yú	动	be good at
9.	满语	Mǎn yǔ	名	Manchu
10.	湖泊	hú pō	名	lake
11.	热闹	rè nao	形	lively
12.	欣赏	xīn shǎng	动	enjoy
13.	一举两得	yì jǔ liǎng dé		kill two birds with one stone
14.	优美	yōu měi	形	graceful
15.	闹中取静	nào zhōng qǔ jìng		enjoy the solitude among excitement
16.	名人	míng rén	名	celebrity
17.	王爷	wáng ye	名	prince
18.	保存	bǎo cún	动	preserve
19.	完整	wán zhěng	形	whole
20.	故居	gù jū	名	former residence
21.	周围	zhōu wéi	名	surrounding
22.	折腾	zhē teng	动	do something over and over again

注释

1. 你不是一直嚷嚷着要看后海吗？
- 嚷 literally means to yell. Here, it means to complain or to nag constantly.

2. "海"是"海"，"海子"是"海子"。
- This is a sentence pattern to emphasize that two things are different. The sea is the sea, a lake is a lake. They are different things.

3. 原来是这样啊。
- Oh, so that's why, that's how it happened. I get it.

4. 这儿既可以喝酒，又可以欣赏美景，一举两得。
- 一举两得 is something like "get two for one" or "kill two birds with one stone". It's not quite the same meaning but roughly that idea.

文化
背景

Hutongs in Beijing

Let's talk a little bit more about hutongs, the narrow alleyways in old Beijing. Many of these have very interesting names, based on different kinds of criteria. Some merely reflect the name of their most prominent occupants, like 赵堂子胡同, which would be where the Zhao family lived. Others have more mysterious names like 羊尾巴胡同, Goat Tail Hutong. We are not sure where that name came from. Other names are very practical, reflecting the dominant trade that would go on in these neighbourhoods, such as 干面胡同, Dry Flour Hutong. One hutong is humorously called 一尺大街. 尺 is a traditional Chinese measurement, like a foot in English. 大街 is the name of a boulevard or major street, but in fact, 一尺大街, this hutong is only about 10 metres long. Note that not all hutongs are actually called "hutong" in their formal name.

Each hutong basically has its own personality. Very few are simply one straight line. The most winding hutong is probably 九道弯, literally 9 turning ways, which actually has over 20 twists and turns. If you come out of that and you still know which way is north, you're doing very well. In Chinese, the expression 找不着北, to not be able to find north, is an expression to indicate that you are completely lost and confused.

Some of the hutongs these days are major streets, others are so narrow that they're not only unpassable by car, but some people would actually have trouble squeezing through. The most narrow hutong, is only 40 cm wide at one point.

The oldest hutong is probably 三庙街, which has a history of over 900 years. Despite the huge changes in Beijing, you can still find these old hutongs today.